ELEPHANT

Female African elephant

POLSKA Zł 7.10 MAMMUTHUS · 30 TYS LAT

Polish stamp showing mammoth

Female Asian elephant

Pot with spout from Thailand

Chinese Ming dynasty jade elephant carving

Wood carving from Thailand of elephant holding lotus bud

Pair of elephant candlesticks

DK EYEWITNESS BOOKS

ELEPHANT

Written by
IAN REDMOND

Photographed by
DAVE KING

Dorling Kindersley

Bronze elephant weights

Asian
elephant

African
elephant

Dorling Kindersley

**LONDON, NEW YORK, AUCKLAND, DELHI,
JOHANNESBURG, MUNICH, PARIS and SYDNEY**

For a full catalog, visit

 www.dk.com

Project editor Christine Webb
Art editor Liz Sephton
Managing editor Helen Parker
Managing art editor Julia Harris
Production Louise Barratt
Picture research Sarah Moule

This Eyewitness ® Book has been conceived by
Dorling Kindersley Limited and Editions Gallimard

© 1993 Dorling Kindersley Limited
This edition © 2000 Dorling Kindersley Limited
First American edition, 1993

Published in the United States by
Dorling Kindersley Publishing, Inc.
95 Madison Avenue
New York, NY 10016
4 6 8 10 9 7 5

Dorling Kindersley books are available at special discounts for bulk
purchases for sales promotions or premiums. Special editions,
including personalized covers, excerpts of existing guides, and
corporate imprints can be created in large quantities for specific
needs. For more information, contact Special Markets Dept., Dorling
Kindersley Publishing, Inc., 95 Madison Ave.,
New York, NY 10016; Fax: (800) 600-9098

Library of Congress Cataloging-in-Publication Data
Redmond, Ian.
Elephant / written by Ian Redmond.
p. cm. — (Eyewitness Books)
Includes index.
Summary: Discusses elephants, their physiology, behavior,
evolution, relatives, uses by humans, and conservation.
1. Elephants — Juvenile literature.
2. Elephants, Fossil — Juvenile literature. [1. Elephants.] I. Series.
QL737.P98R437 2000 599.6'1—dc20 92-20855
ISBN 0-7894-5873-X (pb)
ISBN 0-7894-5872-1 (hc)

Color reproduction by Colourscan, Singapore
Printed in China by Toppan Printing Co. (Shenzhen) Ltd.

19th century
table bell

Balinese elephant
carved from palm
wood

Silver
pin-cushion

Asian
elephant
molar

Contents

Beaten silver elephant
from Cambodia

What is an elephant?

Elephants mean different things to different people. They have been called "nature's masterpiece" and "skilled engineers" as well as "crop-raiding pests," "rogues," and the "sport-hunter's greatest challenge." Elephants are the largest and heaviest living land animals and the most intelligent of domesticated animals. Their noses, gestation period (p. 36), front teeth – and maybe even their memory – are the longest in the animal kingdom. They and their extinct relatives have lived everywhere, except Australia and Antarctica, from sea level to heights of more than 12,000 ft (3,600 m), in habitats ranging from deserts to rain forests to glaciers. In fact, if it were not for humans, elephants would probably rate among the most successful species on Earth.

Illustrators in the 16th century who had probably never seen an elephant, drew them to look like armor-plated monsters

ELEPHANT PAINTING
Asian elephants have a gentle nature and, when tamed, are very tolerant of the things humans do with them. They are worshipped in many human cultures. When used in ceremonial parades and, as in this picture, when taken to be sold at an elephant fair in India, they are sometimes gaily painted.

Forehead has concave center

The total body length of a bull Asian elephant, including trunk and tail, can be as much as 26 ft (8 m)

ASIAN ELEPHANT
The scientific name of the Asian elephant, *Elephas maximus*, means "the biggest elephant," but it is only the second largest species of land animal. A bull (male) Asian elephant might weigh up to 11,900 lb (5,400 kg) and stand 10.5 ft (3.2 m) high at the shoulder. Cows (females) are smaller, weighing up to 9,171 lb (4,160 kg) and standing 8.3 ft (2.5 m) high.

This Asian bull is 49 years old

This Asian cow is eight years old

There are three subspecies (varieties from different regions) of the Asian elephant: Sri Lankan, Indian, and Sumatran

From the tip of its trunk to the tip of its tail, a bull African elephant can measure as much as 30 ft (9 m)

African elephants have larger ears than Asian elephants

ELEPHANT TRACTOR
In 1899, the king of Belgium ordered the founding of an elephant training station in the Belgian Congo (now Zaire). He wanted to use elephants to open up the interior of Africa for trade and development. Forest elephants were (and still are) captured, trained, and used for plowing and for hauling loads (pp. 44–45).

AFRICAN ELEPHANT
The African elephant, *Loxodonta africana,* is the largest animal species living on land today. *Loxodonta* means "lozenge-teeth" and refers to the shape of the ridges on the molars (pp. 22–23). An adult bull African elephant might weigh up to 13,333 lb (6,048 kg) and stand 13.1 ft (4 m) high at the shoulder; females are smaller, weighing up to 7,125 lb (3,232 kg) and measuring up to 8.5 ft (2.6 m) tall. There are two subspecies of the African elephant: this adult bull is a savanna (or bush) elephant, *Loxodonta africana africana.*

ROUND-EARED ELEPHANT
The other subspecies of the African elephant is the forest elephant, *Loxodonta africana cyclotis* (meaning "round ear"), from West and Central Africa. It is smaller than the bush variety and has downward-pointing, brownish tusks and smaller, rounded ears.

SEPARATE SEXES
In elephant society, bulls and cows do not live together in family herds. Instead, bulls spend most of their time alone or in the company of other bulls (pp. 32–33), while cows and calves are normally seen together. Such cow and calf herds are led by an old female, known as the matriarch (pp. 30–31), who is likely to be a grandmother or even a great-grandmother.

The family tree

THE TWO SPECIES OF ELEPHANT alive today represent the topmost branches of an amazing family tree, the other branches of which have all died out. The zoological family Elephantidae, or true elephants, contains at least 26 species. This family is part of a larger group, of more than 160 related species, called the order Proboscidea – meaning animals with a proboscis or trunk. From most fossil remains, we cannot tell what color these animals were, or how much hair or fur covered their bodies. Even the length of the trunk or the size of the ears is open to question, because usually only the hard parts of an animal's body are fossilized. Soft tissues such as skin, muscle, and internal organs are normally eaten by scavengers or simply rot away. By carefully comparing the shapes of fossil teeth, skulls, and other bones, paleontologists (scientists who study fossils) have made reconstructions of many extinct proboscideans. Some of them are shown here.

Extinct proboscideans have featured in stamp designs, such as this *Deinotherium* stamp from Romania

Short trunk

Curved-back tusks in lower jaw are unique and may have been used for digging up roots

DEINOTHERIUM
Deinotherium survived for about 20 million years and became extinct some two million years ago. Although it looks like an elephant, its grinding teeth are so different from those of elephants that some scientists question whether it belongs in the order Proboscidea.

PHIOMIA
Phiomia lived in Africa about 35 million years ago. It stood less than 6.6 ft (2 m) high, and its many elephant-like features included tusks in both upper and lower jaws, and an enlarged skull with air cavities (diploë) that made it light. Relatives of *Phiomia* spread out from Africa across most of the world.

Eyes forward in the skull, unlike elephants

No trunk, but nose-lip probably quite long and flexible

MOERITHERIUM
Moeritherium lived about 50-35 million years ago. It was a pig-sized animal that lived in and around lakes, feeding on water plants. It may not have looked much like an elephant, but its enlarged incisor teeth, some air cavities in the skull, and elephant-like legs lead scientists to believe it was an early branch of the elephant family tree.

Moeritherium fossils are found in Egypt and around the edge of the Sahara, across northern Africa

Tusks are modified upper incisor teeth

Lower jaw is elongated, and short lower tusks reach as far as upper tusks

GOMPHOTHERIUM
Gomphotherium was up to 10 ft (3 m) tall and lived about 20 million years ago. It had an elongated skull and had tusks in both top and bottom jaws. It belongs to the family that includes the "shovel tuskers," whose lower tusks were broad and flat like a shovel. Although most reconstructions show *Gomphotherium* with a trunk like this, not all scientists agree that it had a well-developed trunk, because with its long jaws a trunk would not have been necessary for feeding.

Mongolian stamp showing *Gomphotherium*

THE IMPERIAL MAMMOTH
Mammuthus imperator is the largest of the seven mammoth species known to science. It died out little more than 10,000 years ago. Its remains have been found in North America from Texas to Canada. Standing up to 14 ft (4.2 m) tall, and with phenomenal curved tusks, it must have been an imposing sight striding across the prairies.

Although this reconstruction shows small ears, we cannot be sure of their exact size

STEGODON GANESA
Stegodon ganesa is the most spectacular of the Stegodontidae family, which is similar to but distinct from the true elephants. Its unusual parallel tusks grew so close together that, unless the trunk was very narrow, there was no room for it to move between them. This species, named after the Hindu god Ganesha (pp. 48–49), lived in India. It died out about one million years ago.

Body hair is not shown on any of these models because to include it would only be guesswork

This reconstruction suggests that **Stegodon's** *trunk could only reach its mouth awkwardly around the side of its tusks*

ASIAN ELEPHANT
Studying living elephants, such as this *Elephas maximus,* can give us clues about the behavior and appearance of its ancestors and extinct relatives. By comparing the shape of muscle attachments on bones from an existing species of elephant with those on fossil bones, the shape of the extinct creature can be estimated. But if scientists had only the skull of an African elephant, would they be able to figure out the huge size of its ears?

Sturdy elephant-like legs

Mammoths and mastodons

ROCK ART
More than 15,000 years ago, Stone Age people painted on cave walls pictures of the animals they hunted, including mammoths.

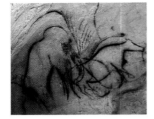

Stone Age painting found in a cave in France

IN 1799, A RUSSIAN FISHERMAN made a startling discovery. Peering into a wall of ice on the banks of the Lena River in Siberia, he could just make out the shape of a massive, shaggy mammoth, apparently staring out at him. He fled in terror. Later, he plucked up the courage to return and chop out the tusks to sell them. Although it is rare to find a whole mammoth, tusks of mammoths are often found in eroding riverbanks in Siberia, and the ivory is still being exported. Woolly mammoths are the most familiar of the elephant's extinct relatives, but early humans lived alongside other relatives of the elephant at the end of the last Ice Age. In the woodlands of eastern North America, mastodons were more common than mammoths. They also may have had a shaggy coat. Whereas mammoths were mainly grazers, eating grass on the plains, mastodons preferred to browse on twigs and leaves. We do not know why mammoths and mastodons became extinct, but computer studies of their decline in numbers suggest that it was a combination of overhunting by humans and changes in the climate that led to their extinction 10,000 years ago.

HAIRY LEGS
Rarely are we able to see the hair, skin, and muscles of long-extinct creatures. Usually only bones and teeth are fossilized, but when frozen mammoths thaw out of the permafrost (permanently frozen ground) in Siberia, we can learn how they looked when alive. This mammoth leg shows the shaggy coat and long "toenails."

SNOW-PLOW TUSKS
Mammoth tusks curved much more than those of the living elephants and were the biggest teeth of any known creature. Some grew to lengths of 16 ft (5 m). Mothers, as in this reconstruction, would have used tusks to protect their calves from predators. Mammoths probably also used them to sweep aside the snow to get at the grasses underneath.

Body squashed flat by weight of frozen earth and snow

FAST-FROZEN MAMMOTH
Perhaps 40,000 years ago, this baby mammoth died in a Siberian marsh just as the ground froze. In 1977, his frozen body was recovered by scientists and nicknamed Dima. One scientist tried to use genes from cells in Dima's best-preserved organs to clone mammoth cells in a test tube. The plan was to implant these cells in a female Asian elephant's womb, in the hope that she would give birth to a bouncing baby mammoth. Unfortunately, it did not work.

A MAMMOTH TASK
The first whole mammoth to be studied by scientists was found in 1900 beside the Berezovka River in Siberia. A shed was built over the thawing carcass while it was excavated and dissected.

WHAT'S THE DIFFERENCE?
Reconstructions of mammoths and mastodons may look alike, but mastodons differ in several ways from mammoths. They are stockier and do not have a steeply sloping back. Some specimens have two small tusks in the lower jaw as well as the big upper tusks.

Mammoths had small ears, which helped to reduce loss of body heat

MAMMOTH ANCESTORS
Mammoths evolved in the cold of the frozen North. But their ancestors originated in what is now the Middle East, 50 million years earlier.

Mammoth stamp from Manama, Bahrain, in the Middle East

IVORY MISSILES
During the Stone Age, ivory was used for making tools, weapons, and household implements. This mammoth-ivory boomerang found in Poland, dates back 23,000 years. The growth lines in the mammoth's tusk show as cones, one inside the other, along the length of the whole tusk.

A long, woolly coat protected mammoths from freezing temperatures

Reconstruction of an adult female mammoth with her baby at her side

Living relatives

ELEPHANTS ARE UNLIKE any other group of animals alive today. To find out how closely elephants are related to other orders of mammals, traditional zoology compares the shapes of bones from living animals and their fossil ancestors. The line is traced back until one fossil is found that could have been the common ancestor of both. Recently, a new technique has provided evidence to confirm (or sometimes confound) the traditional view. Scientists analyze and compare the molecules that make up the bodies of animals. If the molecules are very similar, the animals from which they are taken are likely to be related. One such technique, radioimmunoassay, has verified that three very different groups of mammals – elephants, hyraxes, and sirenians (sea cows) – are related. Their common ancestor lived about 55 million years ago. The aardvark is thought to be the next closest group, having branched off earlier.

MIXED-UP MONSTER
This 16th-century "sea elephant" seems to combine features of an elephant seal, a dugong, and an upside-down walrus. Although it looks like a mythical creature, it may have been drawn from someone's description of a distant sighting of a real animal.

Eyes have a third eyelid, called a nictitating membrane, which acts like goggles underwater

Prehensile, or grasping, upper lip can grab sea grass when feeding. Males have short tusks hidden by the lip

Dugongs have no nails on front flippers

DUGONG: FORK-TAILED SIREN
Sirenians are the only marine mammals to feed mainly on plants. They spend much of their time in shallow water grazing on sea grass, which is why they are also known as sea cows. The peculiarly shaped upper lip and the whale-like tail flukes of dugongs are the best way to tell them from manatees. Dugongs live off coasts and around islands in the southwest Pacific Ocean, from Taiwan to Australia, and westward in the Indian Ocean to the east coast of Africa.

MANATEE: ROUND-TAILED SIREN
There are three species of manatee, one in West Africa, one from Florida to the Caribbean, and one in the Amazon River basin of South America. All but the last live in both fresh water and the sea. They grow to 15 ft (4.6 m) in length and weigh up to 3,550 lb (1,600 kg).

SAILOR'S DREAM
The legends of beautiful mermaids who beckon sailors to a watery grave may have their origin in sightings of manatees. Groups of them often lie on their sides in shallow waters. Glimpsed from afar, or in a mist, they can seem to be part-human.

Long hairs in coat are sensitive to touch, like cat whiskers – such hairs are called vibrissae

Rock hyrax

Round furry ears

THE MIDNIGHT SCREAMER
At nighttime in the forests of Africa, strange sounds such as loud clucks, whistles, piglike squeals, and terrified screams shatter the peace. Few visitors realize that all these eerie noises come from a small, inoffensive-looking mammal called a tree hyrax. On catching a glimpse of one, fewer still would suspect it to be one of the elephants' closest living relatives.

Tree hyrax

ROCK HYRAX *left*
There are several species of hyrax, but it is hard to tell them apart. Tree hyraxes are usually, but not always, in trees; rock hyraxes are usually, but not always, on rocks. All of them resemble a rabbit-sized guinea pig with round furry ears and a tuft of pale hairs in the center of its back. This tuft surrounds a unique dorsal scent gland and stands up when the hyrax is excited or afraid of something. Like elephants, hyraxes are entirely vegetarian, have long incisors that grow throughout their lives, and have similarities in their foot bones.

Dugongs have no hind limbs, only vestigial pelvic bones

Dugongs grow to 13 ft (4 m) in length, and weigh up to 2,000 lb (900 kg)

Donkey-like ears can be folded and closed to keep out biting termites and soldier ants

AARDVARK
Aardvarks are not like any other animal. Zoologists classify them in a separate order, the Tubulidentata – the only living mammalian order with just one species. The name refers to the unique teeth: each composed of 1,000-1,500 tiny tubes made from a substance called dentine. Aardvarks have massive claws for digging and a 1-ft (30-cm) sticky tongue for lapping up termites and ants.

Northern elephant seal calling on the beach in Baja California, Mexico

ELEPHANTINE ANIMALS
Almost any animal with a long nose is likely to be given a common name containing the word "elephant." Male elephant seals have a huge, floppy nose, which they use in courtship displays. Elephant shrews use their mobile pointed snout to rummage through leaf litter in search of insects to eat.

Elephant shrew from Africa

Elephant skeletons

AN ENGINEER looking at an elephant would see that it was built rather like a bridge. There are two columns at each end (the legs) and a curved arch joining them together (the backbone). The backbone supports the hanging weight of the 20 pairs of ribs, the muscles, stomach, and all the other internal organs. All these are heavy, and the leg bones that support their weight are massive. When the elephant stands at rest, the bones in each leg stack one above the other to form a sturdy pillar. This is how an elephant can relax, and even fall asleep, while standing up – and not fall over. In both Asian and African elephants the backbone curves upward in the middle to form a convex shape. Yet, from the side, a living African elephant has a concave dip in its back. This is because the outline of the back is formed by the tops of the spinous processes – the spines that stick out from the main column of the backbone.

ASIAN ROUNDHEADS
An Asian elephant's skull rises to two domes, side by side, on the top of the head. In the male, shown here, the upper jaw juts out much farther than the lower jaw because it contains the roots of the massive tusks.

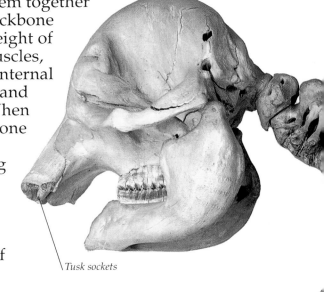

Tusk sockets

Long spines

An Asian elephant has a concave forehead

ASIAN ELEPHANT SKELETON
An Asian elephant usually holds its neck up at an angle of about 45 degrees, so the top of the head is the highest point of the body. The muscles that hold the head up are attached to the back of the skull and to the long spines sticking up from each vertebra. The presence of tusks in this young Asian elephant means that it must be a male, because female Asian elephants seldom have tusks as long as this, even when fully grown.

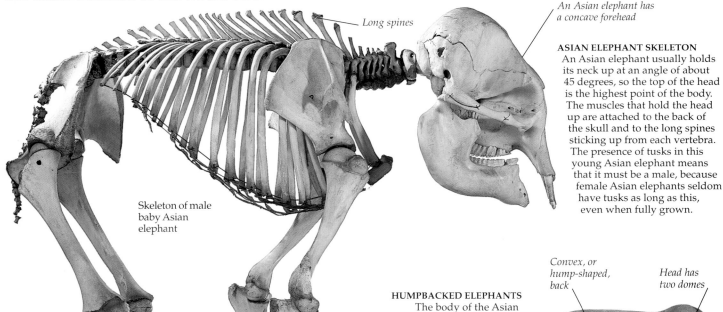

Skeleton of male baby Asian elephant

Convex, or hump-shaped, back

Head has two domes

HUMPBACKED ELEPHANTS
The body of the Asian elephant is shorter and more barrel-shaped than that of the African. By comparing this picture with the skeleton (left), you can see how the length of the spinous processes determines the shape of the back.

Asian elephant

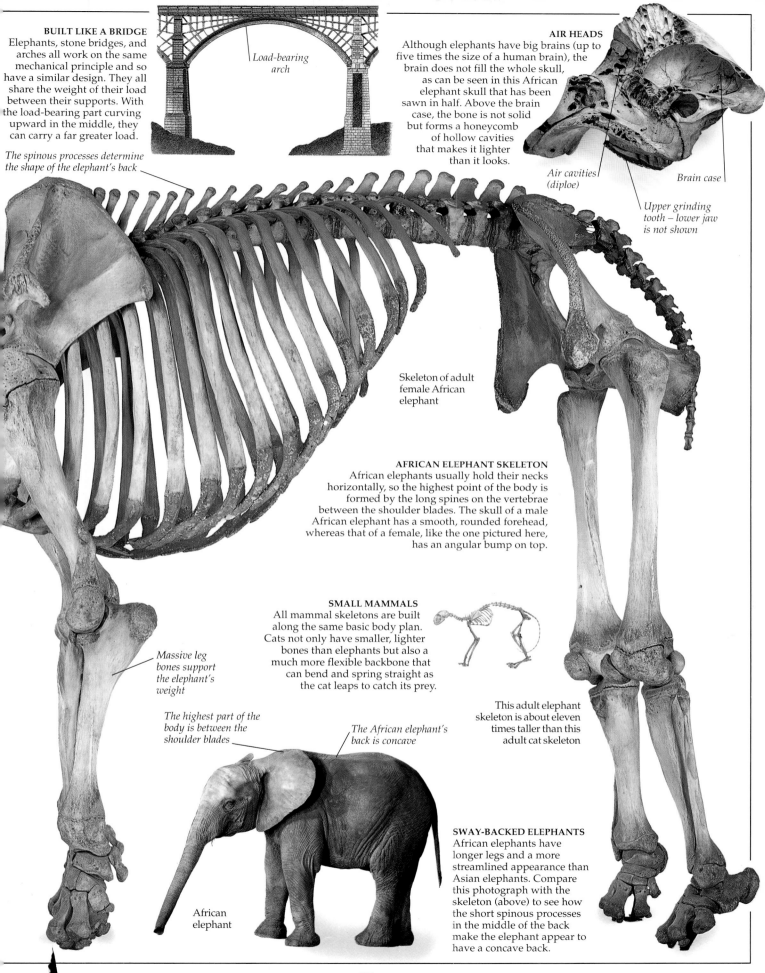

BUILT LIKE A BRIDGE

Elephants, stone bridges, and arches all work on the same mechanical principle and so have a similar design. They all share the weight of their load between their supports. With the load-bearing part curving upward in the middle, they can carry a far greater load.

Load-bearing arch

AIR HEADS

Although elephants have big brains (up to five times the size of a human brain), the brain does not fill the whole skull, as can be seen in this African elephant skull that has been sawn in half. Above the brain case, the bone is not solid but forms a honeycomb of hollow cavities that makes it lighter than it looks.

Air cavities (diploe)

Brain case

Upper grinding tooth – lower jaw is not shown

The spinous processes determine the shape of the elephant's back

Skeleton of adult female African elephant

AFRICAN ELEPHANT SKELETON

African elephants usually hold their necks horizontally, so the highest point of the body is formed by the long spines on the vertebrae between the shoulder blades. The skull of a male African elephant has a smooth, rounded forehead, whereas that of a female, like the one pictured here, has an angular bump on top.

SMALL MAMMALS

All mammal skeletons are built along the same basic body plan. Cats not only have smaller, lighter bones than elephants but also a much more flexible backbone that can bend and spring straight as the cat leaps to catch its prey.

Massive leg bones support the elephant's weight

This adult elephant skeleton is about eleven times taller than this adult cat skeleton

The highest part of the body is between the shoulder blades

The African elephant's back is concave

African elephant

SWAY-BACKED ELEPHANTS

African elephants have longer legs and a more streamlined appearance than Asian elephants. Compare this photograph with the skeleton (above) to see how the short spinous processes in the middle of the back make the elephant appear to have a concave back.

15

Elephants on tiptoe

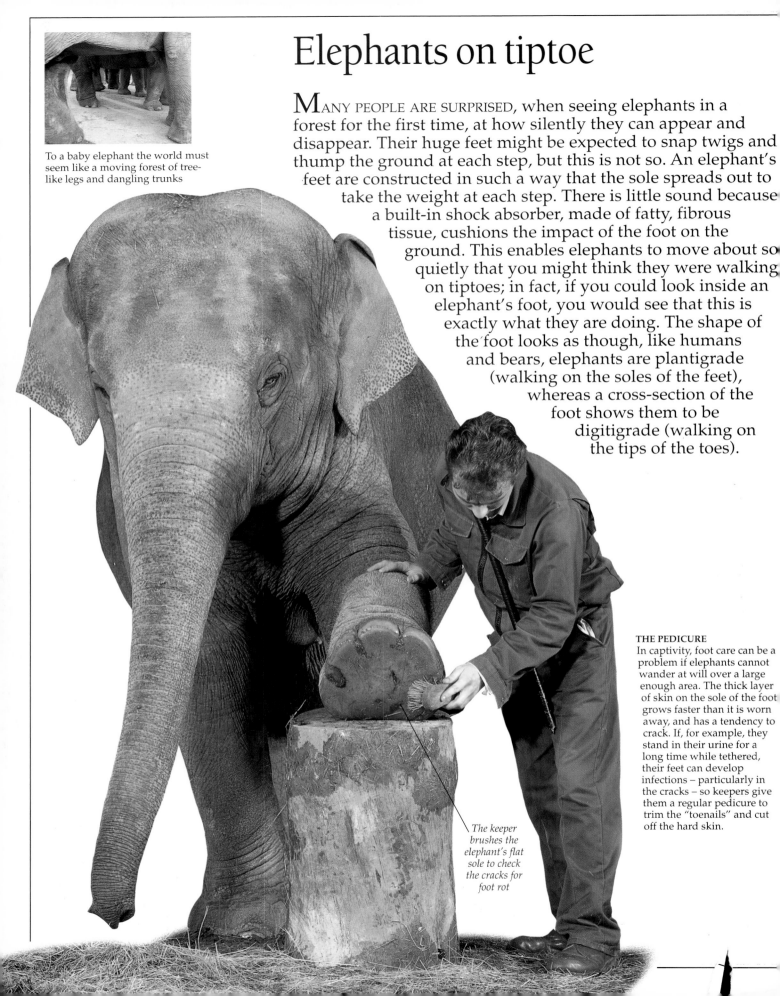

To a baby elephant the world must seem like a moving forest of tree-like legs and dangling trunks

MANY PEOPLE ARE SURPRISED, when seeing elephants in a forest for the first time, at how silently they can appear and disappear. Their huge feet might be expected to snap twigs and thump the ground at each step, but this is not so. An elephant's feet are constructed in such a way that the sole spreads out to take the weight at each step. There is little sound because a built-in shock absorber, made of fatty, fibrous tissue, cushions the impact of the foot on the ground. This enables elephants to move about so quietly that you might think they were walking on tiptoes; in fact, if you could look inside an elephant's foot, you would see that this is exactly what they are doing. The shape of the foot looks as though, like humans and bears, elephants are plantigrade (walking on the soles of the feet), whereas a cross-section of the foot shows them to be digitigrade (walking on the tips of the toes).

THE PEDICURE
In captivity, foot care can be a problem if elephants cannot wander at will over a large enough area. The thick layer of skin on the sole of the foot grows faster than it is worn away, and has a tendency to crack. If, for example, they stand in their urine for a long time while tethered, their feet can develop infections – particularly in the cracks – so keepers give them a regular pedicure to trim the "toenails" and cut off the hard skin.

The keeper brushes the elephant's flat sole to check the cracks for foot rot

INSIDE VIEW

An elephant's weight rests on the tip of each toe and on the fibrous cushion under the "heel." The hoof-like nails are attached to the skin in front of each toe bone, not to the bone itself. They are made of keratin, the same fibrous protein that hair is made of.

Internal structure of an elephant's foot

Toe bone

Tip of toe

"Heel" cushion

HANDY FEET

Elephants have flat-soled, almost circular front feet – the equivalent of the human hand. There are normally five "toenails" on each forefoot in both species of elephant (although some African elephants have only four "toenails" on the forefoot). As each foot is put down, the whole foot expands under the weight.

As foot is lifted, toes sag and foot diameter is reduced

As foot is put down, toes spread and diameter of foot increases

Cracks and ridges on soles of feet give elephants a good grip

GETTING A GRIP

Elephants are very good climbers of steep hills, mountains, and even cliffs on occasion. Like humans who go barefoot, the skin on the soles of an elephant's feet is thicker than usual. This skin and the "toenails" are constantly worn down by the amount of walking that elephants do in the wild. The sole skin is not normally worn smooth, but has cracks and ridges that make a pattern not unlike the cleats on a walking or climbing boot. The function is the same in both cases – to get a grip when climbing rocks or going over rough ground.

WALKING BOOT

Humans imitate nature by wearing boots with ridged soles, like stylized elephant feet, when walking or climbing over the kind of ground an elephant just takes in its stride.

HIGH-PRESSURE WOMEN

An average-sized woman wearing stiletto heels exerts more pressure per square inch on the ground than an average elephant – even when the elephant is standing on one leg! A five-ton elephant standing on one front leg would not dent a wooden floor, whereas a woman of average weight wearing stiletto heels does dent floors.

FOOTPRINTS IN THE SAND

An elephant walking along often sets its hind foot in the track of the forefoot. However, if the circumference of a clear circular forefoot print can be measured, the elephant's approximate height can be calculated by multiplying by two.

OVAL FEET

The spread of toes is less obvious when the hind foot takes the elephant's weight. The sole has an oval cross section and, as a rule, only four "toenails." Contrary to popular belief, the number of "toenails" is not necessarily different in the two species.

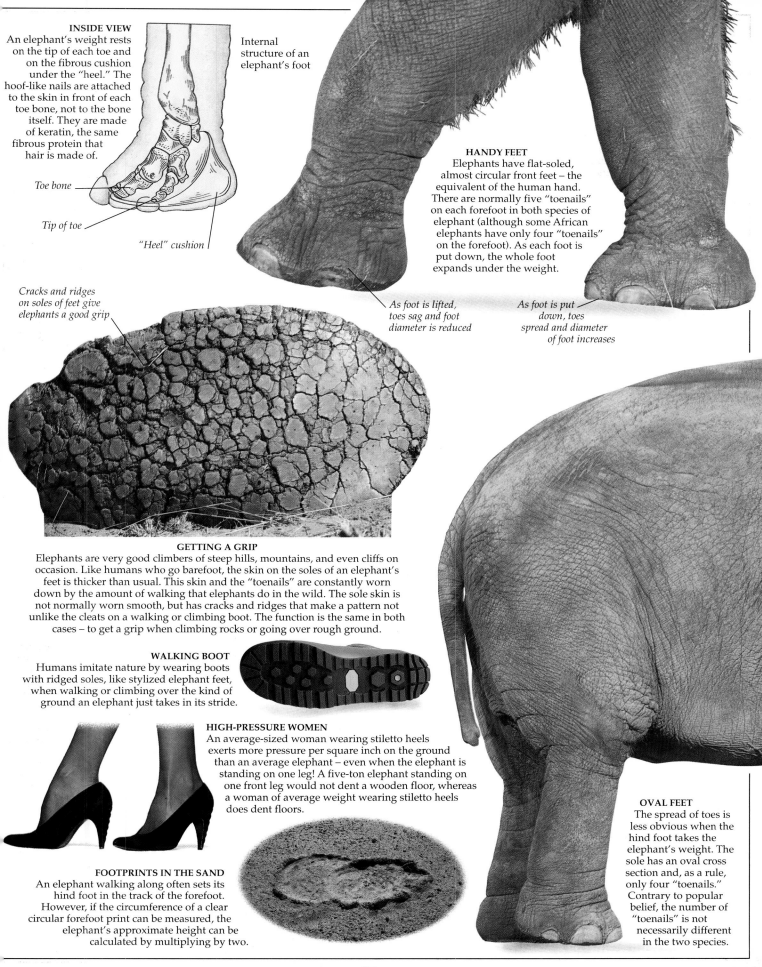

The hand-nose

IMAGINE WHAT IT WOULD BE LIKE if your nostrils ran down inside your arm to emerge between your thumb and forefinger. Just think of the things you could do. You could stretch your nose to sniff around corners! Choosing food would be easy – just sniff and touch to test if it is ripe, then pick it up and pop it into your mouth. The elephant's trunk enables it to do all these things and more. It can do almost all the things humans do with a hand and nose as well as lips and facial muscles. The incredible trunk can also draw up water and pour it down the elephant's throat, blow it over its body, or squirt it playfully at a friend. In short, it is the most versatile organ in the animal kingdom.

FLEXIBLE TENTACLES
Almost every animal with legs or arms has some sort of skeleton to strengthen and support its limbs. But a skeleton can only move in the way the joints allow. Only animals with tentacles, such as an octopus or a sea anemone, have limbs that can curl and bend in any direction like an elephant's trunk.

NOT JUST A LONG NOSE
The trunk is made up of the nose, upper lip, and muscles of the elephant's face, joined together and lengthened to form a unique fifth limb. There are no bones down the middle, which is why an elephant can move its trunk in any direction, as when signaling. If two elephants meet, one may raise its trunk, and then curl it back to touch its forehead. This is thought to be a sign to acknowledge that the other elephant is dominant (has a higher social position) over the one who is signaling.

EYE WIPER
If an elephant gets something in its eye, it delicately uses its trunk to wipe it away. It might wipe with its trunk-finger or, as this African elephant is doing, with the back of its trunk tip, just as we might use the back of our hand to rub an eye.

TRUNK-WRESTLING CHAMPIONSHIPS
During trials of strength between bull elephants, the sparring partners will push, clash tusks, and grapple with each other using their trunks. Such mock battles are usually good-natured affairs.

IVORY TRUNK-REST
Sometimes the muscles holding up the trunk get tired. Elephants with forward-curving tusks often drape their trunk over one of these convenient ivory shelves when it is not in use.

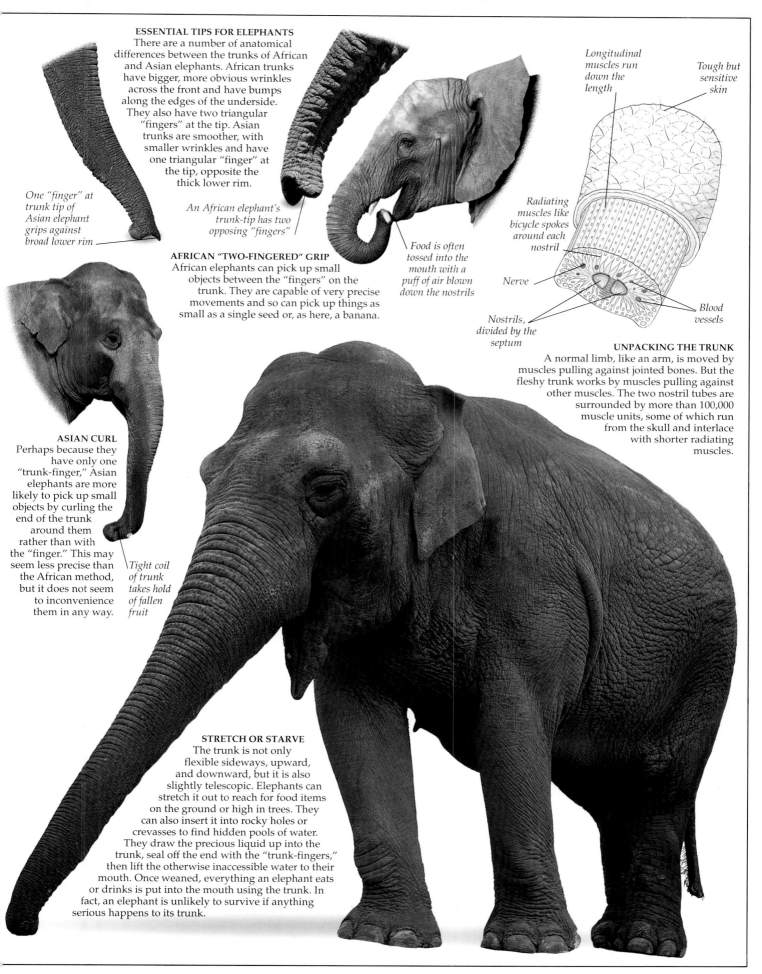

ESSENTIAL TIPS FOR ELEPHANTS
There are a number of anatomical differences between the trunks of African and Asian elephants. African trunks have bigger, more obvious wrinkles across the front and have bumps along the edges of the underside. They also have two triangular "fingers" at the tip. Asian trunks are smoother, with smaller wrinkles and have one triangular "finger" at the tip, opposite the thick lower rim.

One "finger" at trunk tip of Asian elephant grips against broad lower rim

An African elephant's trunk-tip has two opposing "fingers"

AFRICAN "TWO-FINGERED" GRIP
African elephants can pick up small objects between the "fingers" on the trunk. They are capable of very precise movements and so can pick up things as small as a single seed or, as here, a banana.

Food is often tossed into the mouth with a puff of air blown down the nostrils

Longitudinal muscles run down the length

Tough but sensitive skin

Radiating muscles like bicycle spokes around each nostril

Nerve

Nostrils, divided by the septum

Blood vessels

UNPACKING THE TRUNK
A normal limb, like an arm, is moved by muscles pulling against jointed bones. But the fleshy trunk works by muscles pulling against other muscles. The two nostril tubes are surrounded by more than 100,000 muscle units, some of which run from the skull and interlace with shorter radiating muscles.

ASIAN CURL
Perhaps because they have only one "trunk-finger," Asian elephants are more likely to pick up small objects by curling the end of the trunk around them rather than with the "finger." This may seem less precise than the African method, but it does not seem to inconvenience them in any way.

Tight coil of trunk takes hold of fallen fruit

STRETCH OR STARVE
The trunk is not only flexible sideways, upward, and downward, but it is also slightly telescopic. Elephants can stretch it out to reach for food items on the ground or high in trees. They can also insert it into rocky holes or crevasses to find hidden pools of water. They draw the precious liquid up into the trunk, seal off the end with the "trunk-fingers," then lift the otherwise inaccessible water to their mouth. Once weaned, everything an elephant eats or drinks is put into the mouth using the trunk. In fact, an elephant is unlikely to survive if anything serious happens to its trunk.

Tool-teeth

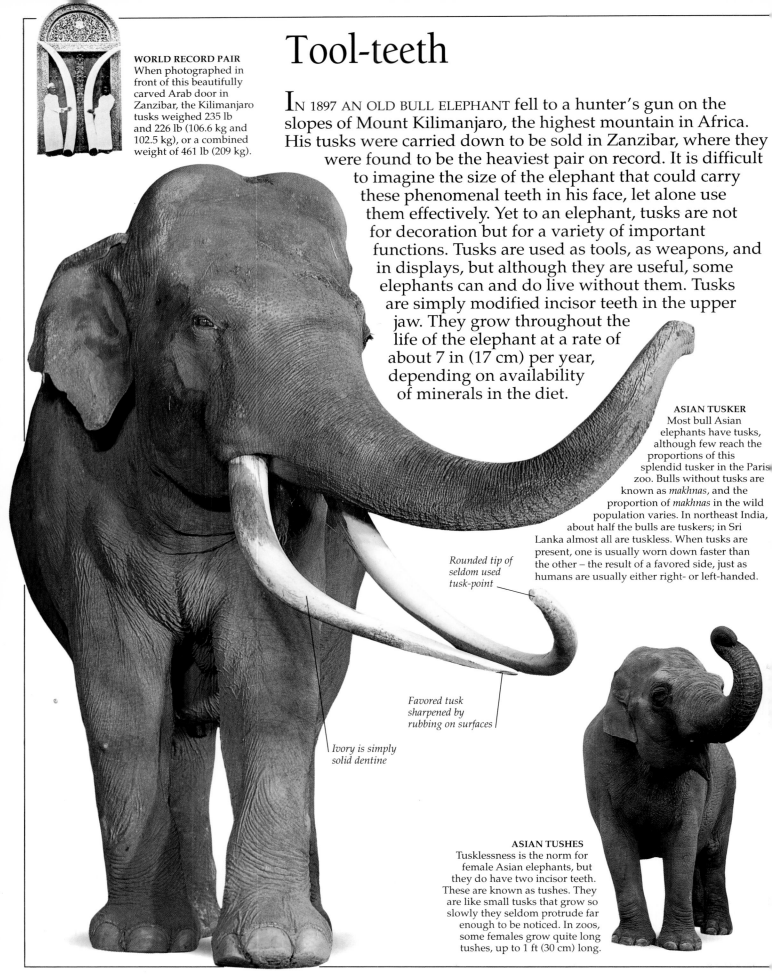

WORLD RECORD PAIR
When photographed in front of this beautifully carved Arab door in Zanzibar, the Kilimanjaro tusks weighed 235 lb and 226 lb (106.6 kg and 102.5 kg), or a combined weight of 461 lb (209 kg).

IN 1897 AN OLD BULL ELEPHANT fell to a hunter's gun on the slopes of Mount Kilimanjaro, the highest mountain in Africa. His tusks were carried down to be sold in Zanzibar, where they were found to be the heaviest pair on record. It is difficult to imagine the size of the elephant that could carry these phenomenal teeth in his face, let alone use them effectively. Yet to an elephant, tusks are not for decoration but for a variety of important functions. Tusks are used as tools, as weapons, and in displays, but although they are useful, some elephants can and do live without them. Tusks are simply modified incisor teeth in the upper jaw. They grow throughout the life of the elephant at a rate of about 7 in (17 cm) per year, depending on availability of minerals in the diet.

ASIAN TUSKER
Most bull Asian elephants have tusks, although few reach the proportions of this splendid tusker in the Paris zoo. Bulls without tusks are known as *makhnas*, and the proportion of *makhnas* in the wild population varies. In northeast India, about half the bulls are tuskers; in Sri Lanka almost all are tuskless. When tusks are present, one is usually worn down faster than the other – the result of a favored side, just as humans are usually either right- or left-handed.

Rounded tip of seldom used tusk-point

Favored tusk sharpened by rubbing on surfaces

Ivory is simply solid dentine

ASIAN TUSHES
Tusklessness is the norm for female Asian elephants, but they do have two incisor teeth. These are known as tushes. They are like small tusks that grow so slowly they seldom protrude far enough to be noticed. In zoos, some females grow quite long tushes, up to 1 ft (30 cm) long.

This elephant had four tusks, but elephants with up to seven tusks have been recorded

TOOTH PICKS

Elephant tusks are shaped rather like a pickax without the handle, and they are often used like one. But rather than swing the tusk like a pickax, elephants are more likely to place the point carefully, then lean their body-weight on it, until it sinks into the earth or rock.

STRANGE BUT TRUE

For years, Pygmies in the Ituri Forest, central Africa, spoke of a powerful and dangerous old elephant bull with four tusks. Few outsiders believed in this legendary Elephant King until its skull and all four tusks – the result of a rare deformity in both roots – were finally located.

ROADSIDE TUSKINGS

The signs of salt-hungry elephants can be seen on roadside cuttings in eastern Africa's mountain forests. Smooth curves have been gouged out of this cutting by tuskers wanting to sample the exposed soil for possibly useful minerals.

AFRICAN TUSKER

When this huge tusker was born, he already had tiny 2-in (5-cm) deciduous tusks (equivalent to milk teeth). They would have been replaced by his permanent tusks at 6-13 months of age. At first his new tusks had a cap of enamel, but this would soon have worn away to leave tusks of solid dentine.

SMALL ASIAN MALE

An Asian elephant's tusk has relatively thin, near-parallel sides, gradually tapering to a point. The record length for an Asian tusk is 10 ft (3.02 m), but the record weight for a single Asian tusk is only 86 lb (39 kg).

Tusk enters skull here

TUSKED TO DEATH

Tusks can be used as deadly weapons against predators. This ability was put to use by warring humans when elephants were trained to take part in human conflict, as shown in this 17th-century Indian illustration. As long ago as the days of the Roman circuses, enraged elephants were pitted against gladiators.

SLENDER AFRICAN FEMALE *above*

Tusks from female African elephants are slender and almost parallel for most of their length. About one third of the total length is embedded in the alveolus, or socket, in the skull. Inside this part is a conical pulp cavity, rich in blood vessels and in nerves sensitive to pressure.

MAMMOTH IVORY

Mammoth tusks have a more pronounced curve and, depending on their state of preservation, are often deeply stained. The female's tusks are smaller and more parallel than the male's and are less tapered.

The record for the heaviest single African tusk is 259 lb (117 kg), and the longest single tusk measures 11 ft 6 in (3.45 m)

BIG AFRICAN BULL

Tusks from male African elephants are much thicker than those from females. This is probably the result of sexual selection, since the male with the biggest tusks is most likely to breed (pp. 32–33).

Unusual teeth

No other animal has teeth like an elephant. They are different in their size and shape and in the way they grow. The tusks are the elephant's only front teeth. They grow continuously and do not normally wear out. The side teeth, however, which grind up the elephant's rough food, do wear out and are replaced six times in the elephant's lifetime. Humans, like most mammals, have two sets of teeth in their lifetime. By the time a person stops growing, at about 20 years of age, he or she will have a complete second set of teeth (although the last molars, or wisdom teeth, sometimes take longer). A 20-year-old elephant, on the other hand, will already be well into its fourth set of teeth. An elephant starts out with a set of four side teeth, one in each corner of the upper and lower jaws. As the elephant grows, the teeth move forward and a new set of slightly bigger teeth emerges. Unlike the teeth of humans, which erupt from the jaw in their final place, elephant teeth erupt from the back and move along the jaw toward the front. Each tooth gets more and more worn as it moves forward, but by the time the last bits drop out, it has been completely replaced by the tooth behind it, much as if the teeth were on a very slow conveyor belt.

A THORNY PROBLEM
The huge, sharp thorns of acacia trees are no defense against an elephant. Carefully avoiding the thorns with her trunk, this African elephant has torn off a branch and is removing the bark with her molars.

JAWBONE
This left half of an African elephant's jawbone has had the bone chipped away to reveal the roots of the teeth. The big tooth is molar 5, but the last bit of molar 4 is still in use. The round lump in the angle of the jaw is the beginning of molar 6.

Molar 6

Molar 5 is good for about 20 years of chewing

Molar 6

Roots deep in jawbone

Human molar

African elephant molar has diamond-shaped ridges

Asian elephant molar has parallel ridges

TEETH RIDGES
An elephant molar is made up of several plates, or lamellae, stuck together. The enamel top of each molar wears down as it grinds on its opposite tooth, revealing a diamond shape in African elephants and thin parallel ridges in Asian elephants.

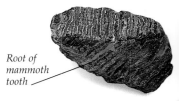

Root of mammoth tooth

MAMMOTH TOOTH
Fossil mammoth teeth are sometimes dredged up from the bottom of the North Sea. The ridges on the grinding surface are more like those of an Asian elephant than an African.

The last molar is bigger than a brick and appears when the elephant is about 40 years old

SET OF TEETH
When an elephant dies, the size of its teeth, and the amount of wear on them, enable scientists to work out how long it lived. These six teeth come from five different African elephants, ranging from a tiny calf to an adult of more than 50 years.

Molar 5

Only the first five ridges of molar 5 have come into use

Molar 4

Molar 4 is almost worn out. It comes from the same elephant as molar 5

Molar 3

Molar 3 usually lasts from about three and a half to about nine years of age

Molar 2

Molar 2 usually erupts before the age of 18 months

Molar 1

Molar 1 is present in newborn babies

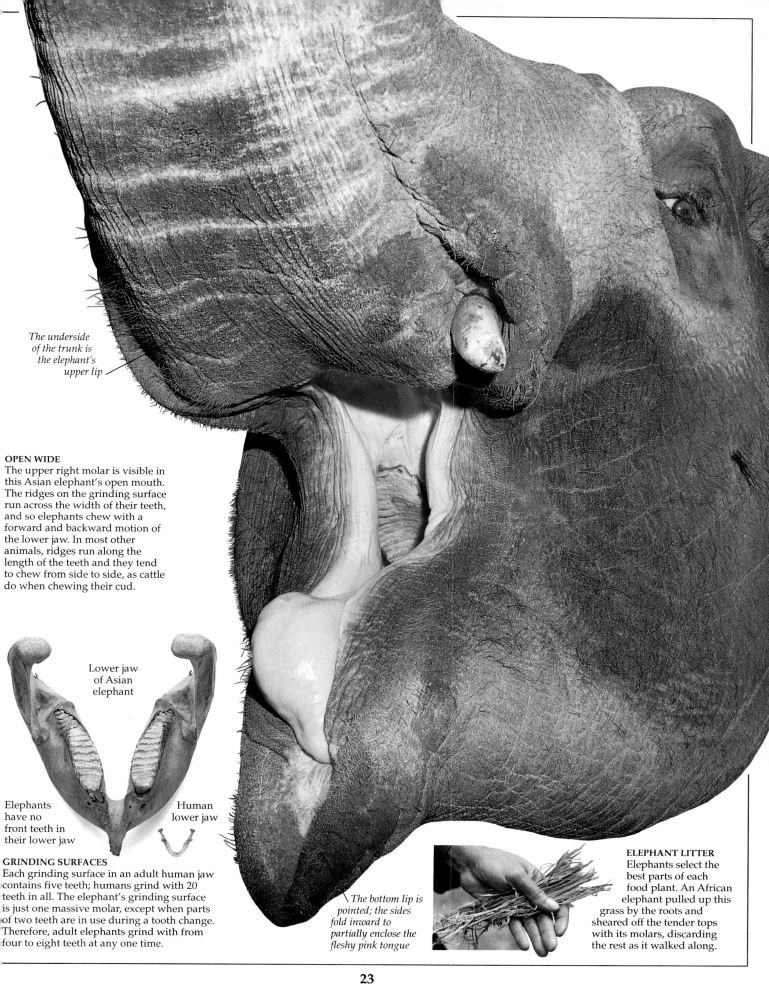

*The underside
of the trunk is
the elephant's
upper lip*

OPEN WIDE
The upper right molar is visible in
this Asian elephant's open mouth.
The ridges on the grinding surface
run across the width of their teeth,
and so elephants chew with a
forward and backward motion of
the lower jaw. In most other
animals, ridges run along the
length of the teeth and they tend
to chew from side to side, as cattle
do when chewing their cud.

Lower jaw
of Asian
elephant

Elephants
have no
front teeth in
their lower jaw

Human
lower jaw

GRINDING SURFACES
Each grinding surface in an adult human jaw
contains five teeth; humans grind with 20
teeth in all. The elephant's grinding surface
is just one massive molar, except when parts
of two teeth are in use during a tooth change.
Therefore, adult elephants grind with from
four to eight teeth at any one time.

*The bottom lip is
pointed; the sides
fold inward to
partially enclose the
fleshy pink tongue*

ELEPHANT LITTER
Elephants select the
best parts of each
food plant. An African
elephant pulled up this
grass by the roots and
sheared off the tender tops
with its molars, discarding
the rest as it walked along.

Nonstop dining

Elephants spend about three quarters of their time, day and night, selecting, picking, preparing, and eating food. An adult elephant in the wild will eat in the region of 220 to 440 lb (100 to 200 kg) of vegetation per day, depending on the habitat and the size of the elephant. Elephants are herbivores (plant eaters), but they cannot digest cellulose, the substance that makes up much of plant matter. Unlike ruminants, such as cows and other animals that chew the cud, elephants do not have extra chambers in their stomach to aid digestion. They do, however, have a very large cecum – a bag-like organ where the small intestine joins onto the large intestine. Millions of protozoa (amoebalike organisms) and bacteria live in the cecum. They feed on the part digested vegetation and in turn are digested by the elephant when they die. Even so, elephant dung is full of bulky plant fibers and seeds that have passed through the elephant virtually intact.

UP TO HIS EARS IN DINNER
In both species of elephant 30-60 percent of the diet is grass, if it is available (they eat less in dry seasons and more in the wet). Elephants that dwell in forests go out of their way to search for grassy glades. Swamps, such as this one in a Sumatran national park, are ideal locations for a delicious grassy meal.

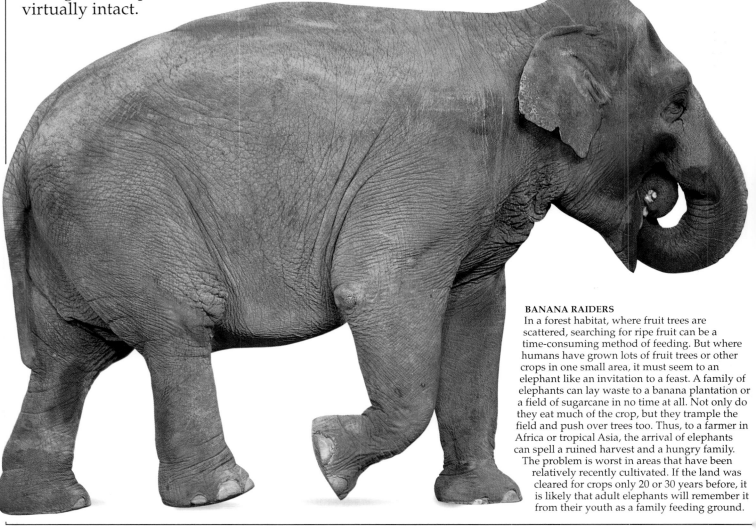

BANANA RAIDERS
In a forest habitat, where fruit trees are scattered, searching for ripe fruit can be a time-consuming method of feeding. But where humans have grown lots of fruit trees or other crops in one small area, it must seem to an elephant like an invitation to a feast. A family of elephants can lay waste to a banana plantation or a field of sugarcane in no time at all. Not only do they eat much of the crop, but they trample the field and push over trees too. Thus, to a farmer in Africa or tropical Asia, the arrival of elephants can spell a ruined harvest and a hungry family. The problem is worst in areas that have been relatively recently cultivated. If the land was cleared for crops only 20 or 30 years before, it is likely that adult elephants will remember it from their youth as a family feeding ground.

REACH FOR THE SKY

With their trunk and tusks, elephants are equipped to reach up or dig for many different kinds of food. Like humans and apes, an elephant's choice of food plants will be determined partly by what grows locally, partly by what was learned from its mother, and partly by what it has discovered by trying novel food items. The number of plant species eaten by any one elephant may vary but is likely to be more than fifty.

STRAW STUFFING

As well as choosing food-plants for taste and nutritious quality, elephants select their meals by the time it takes to prepare each mouthful. Eating long grass is probably the easiest and quickest way for an elephant to fill up. Asian elephants coil their trunk around a tussock of grass (African elephants use their "trunk-fingers") and pull. Then they knock off the soil from the roots, if they are edible, and stuff the bundle in their mouth for a brief chew while preparing the next trunkful.

WANTED: ELEPHANT SCARECROW

These Sumatran farmers are trying to chase elephants out of their cornfields. As the human population grows and more elephant habitat is cleared for cultivation, conflict between farmers and elephants increases. The problem can be eased by electric fences or elephant-proof ditches, but both are expensive.

BARK CHEWING

One of the most time-consuming food items for elephants to prepare is bark. Branches or saplings up to the thickness of a man's leg can be broken off and the bark stripped away in the mouth (left). With larger trees, the elephant drives a tusk between the bark and the sapwood, then it yanks a strip off the tree with its trunk. The soft wood of the baobab tree (above) is also eaten. Such tusking sometimes destroys the whole tree.

TREE PRUNING

When elephants browse on trees and bushes, they do not just pluck leaves like most other herbivores. Leaves, twigs, and even small branches are pulled off, ground up, and swallowed. This acts like pruning and causes the bushes to grow back thicker than before. In the wet season in Uganda, up to 42 percent of the elephants' diet was found to be taken from trees and bushes. However, in the dry season when the grass was less nutritious, this rose to as much as 67 percent, probably because the trees, with deeper roots, stay green for longer.

Playtime in the bath

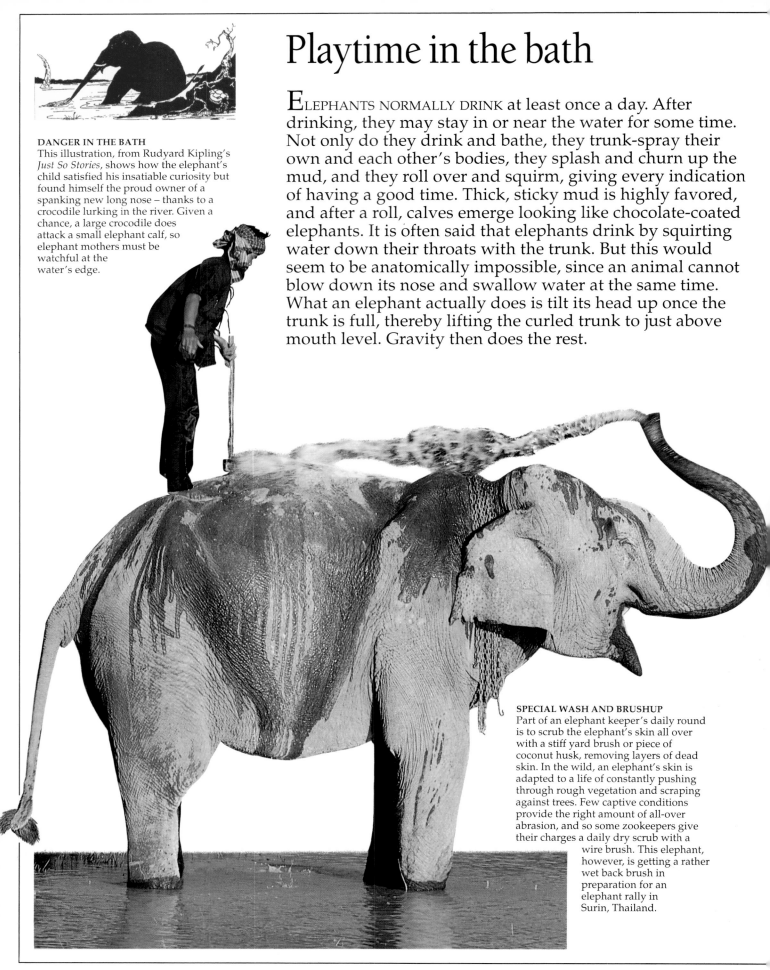

ELEPHANTS NORMALLY DRINK at least once a day. After drinking, they may stay in or near the water for some time. Not only do they drink and bathe, they trunk-spray their own and each other's bodies, they splash and churn up the mud, and they roll over and squirm, giving every indication of having a good time. Thick, sticky mud is highly favored, and after a roll, calves emerge looking like chocolate-coated elephants. It is often said that elephants drink by squirting water down their throats with the trunk. But this would seem to be anatomically impossible, since an animal cannot blow down its nose and swallow water at the same time. What an elephant actually does is tilt its head up once the trunk is full, thereby lifting the curled trunk to just above mouth level. Gravity then does the rest.

DANGER IN THE BATH
This illustration, from Rudyard Kipling's *Just So Stories*, shows how the elephant's child satisfied his insatiable curiosity but found himself the proud owner of a spanking new long nose – thanks to a crocodile lurking in the river. Given a chance, a large crocodile does attack a small elephant calf, so elephant mothers must be watchful at the water's edge.

SPECIAL WASH AND BRUSHUP
Part of an elephant keeper's daily round is to scrub the elephant's skin all over with a stiff yard brush or piece of coconut husk, removing layers of dead skin. In the wild, an elephant's skin is adapted to a life of constantly pushing through rough vegetation and scraping against trees. Few captive conditions provide the right amount of all-over abrasion, and so some zookeepers give their charges a daily dry scrub with a wire brush. This elephant, however, is getting a rather wet back brush in preparation for an elephant rally in Surin, Thailand.

SUBMARINE ELEPHANTS

Elephants can swim very well over distances of up to several miles; they will even play in the sea if their range includes some coastline with elephant habitat next door. They churn along in the water quite effectively and are not too concerned about staying at the surface. If they need to breathe, they simply use their trunk as a snorkel. If they are crossing a fast-flowing river, cows will position their calves on the upstream side to keep them from being swept away.

FIRST QUENCH THE THIRST...

These two young bulls are busily pouring one or two dozen trunkfuls of water down their throats. Each trunkful may amount to a gallon or two (4-5 liters). An adult elephant will drink about 60 gallons (225 liters) of water per day, and this can sometimes be drunk during a single visit. The elephant's head is always tilted up when drinking, so the fluid can run down its throat.

...NEXT CHURN UP THE MUD...

It is quite common to see an elephant change a clear water-hole into a cloudy, mud-filled pool. One forefoot is raised and repeatedly splashed backward and forward in the same spot, churning up clouds of sediment. Young elephants watch with interest, and often try it for themselves but with less success. Whenever a herd emerges from a pool, a watermark usually shows how deep they have ventured in.

BATH TIME FOR WORKING ELEPHANTS

Domesticated elephants soon get into a regular routine and show distinct signs of looking forward to their daily bath. They head down to the riverbank at a fast walk, knowing that the day's work is done and that an enormous meal will be waiting for them later. The mood is captured in this painting showing elephants bathing in Sri Lanka.

...THEN GO SNORKELING!

Young elephants sometimes get out of their depth in their efforts to stay beside their mother. With its snorkel, however, even a small baby can gain a little extra depth by holding up its trunk to breathe while totally submerged. Very young calves, who have yet to master the art of drinking with the trunk, just dunk their faces in and drink directly through the mouth.

Keeping cool

Out on the African savanna, the flat-topped acacia tree offers shelter from the heat of the noonday sun

ELEPHANTS HAVE A PROBLEM keeping cool. As in all animals, some heat is generated when they move their muscles – this is why people doing exercises soon begin to feel hot. Overheated humans lose their excess heat by sweating; the surface of the skin is cooled as the sweat evaporates. Elephants, however, do not appear to have sweat glands in their skin. Biologists examining sections of elephant skin have never found sweat glands, though they know that water is lost through the skin. However, even if they did have sweat glands, they would not lose enough heat from the skin to cool their massive bodies. Small animals have a much greater surface area in proportion to their volume than large animals, and so small animals can lose heat through their skin more easily (pp. 38–39). To lose heat, elephants must actively do something. If they are near water, they might give themselves a cold shower with their trunk; if they are near trees, they move into the shade; if they can find or make some mud, they plaster it all over themselves; if there is no water for mud, dry dust will do – elephants are often seen throwing dust over themselves to form a protective layer on the skin. In addition to all these actions, elephants flap their ears to keep cool.

IN THE SHADE
Forest-dwelling elephants, like this Asian elephant in Sumatra, spend most of their lives in the shade. Very little sunlight shines through the canopy of the trees, and so the air temperature is several degrees cooler than in a sunny glade or out on the savanna.

Elephants love to wallow and roll in mud, which helps to protect their skin from the heat

BUILT-IN SHOWER HOSE
Wherever an elephant wanders, it can always take a shower by squirting a trunkful of water over itself. With practice, elephants can reach every bit of their body by swinging the trunk and blowing at just the right time.

COOL WRINKLES
Elephants look as though their skin is several sizes too big, but all those wrinkles help to keep them cool. Wrinkles increase the surface area, so there is more skin to wet when bathing. Also, the cracks and crevices trap moisture, which then takes much longer to evaporate. Thus, a wrinkly elephant keeps cooler for longer than it would with smooth skin.

MUD, MUD, GLORIOUS MUD
The color of an elephant depends on the color of the local mud. Because elephants so love to get thoroughly plastered with mud, their typical grayish brown skin color is seldom seen. Instead, people on safari are surprised to see red, gray, black, or even yellow elephants emerging from their wallows. Each elephant carries away several pounds of mud on its body, and in this way, water holes get bigger and bigger over the years.

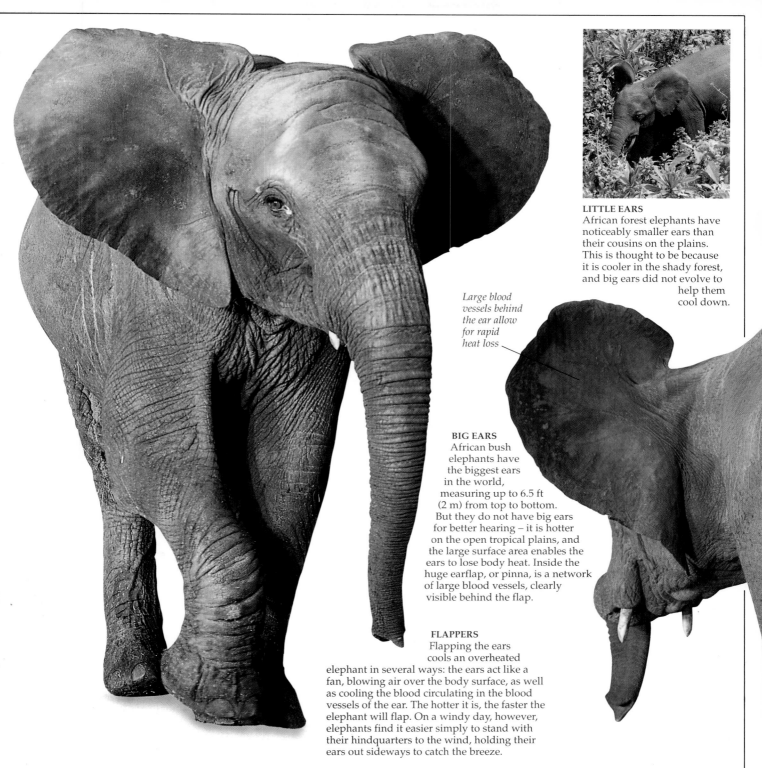

LITTLE EARS

African forest elephants have noticeably smaller ears than their cousins on the plains. This is thought to be because it is cooler in the shady forest, and big ears did not evolve to help them cool down.

Large blood vessels behind the ear allow for rapid heat loss

BIG EARS

African bush elephants have the biggest ears in the world, measuring up to 6.5 ft (2 m) from top to bottom. But they do not have big ears for better hearing – it is hotter on the open tropical plains, and the large surface area enables the ears to lose body heat. Inside the huge earflap, or pinna, is a network of large blood vessels, clearly visible behind the flap.

FLAPPERS

Flapping the ears cools an overheated elephant in several ways: the ears act like a fan, blowing air over the body surface, as well as cooling the blood circulating in the blood vessels of the ear. The hotter it is, the faster the elephant will flap. On a windy day, however, elephants find it easier simply to stand with their hindquarters to the wind, holding their ears out sideways to catch the breeze.

DUSTERS

With a well-aimed trunkful of soil, this African bush elephant is coating her back with a layer of dust. On the savanna, where there is little shade, it will keep the sun from burning her skin. The coat of dust may also serve to discourage biting insects. By watching how the plumes of dust drift, elephant observers can see which way the wind is blowing and can remain undetected by keeping downwind.

OTHER WAYS TO COOL IT

Like elephants, dogs and birds do not sweat. Instead, they open their mouths and pant, taking short breaths to cool themselves off. Dogs also let their long wet tongues hang out to cool by evaporation.

She who must be obeyed

Like human children, young elephants sometimes learn the rules of their society from a nanny or babysitter

THE EXPRESSION "MOTHER KNOWS BEST" would fit well into elephant society. Family herds are not led by a massive bull but by an old grandmother known as the matriarch. She is the dominant female, and the herd she is in charge of will probably consist of her sisters, daughters, female cousins, and their young offspring. Because elephants live to such a great age – possibly as long as 70 years – their social ties last for decades. Anyone watching a big family herd will probably notice that the larger herd is divided up into small subgroups of three to six elephants. These are the basic units of elephant society, usually made up of a mother and her calves, perhaps staying close to her sister and her sister's offspring.

The mind of the matriarch contains local elephant lore handed down through generations

FEMALE LEADER
As leader of the family, the matriarch is responsible for the herd's safety and for providing enough food and water. She therefore has to decide how far and in which direction they should go in their constant search for new pastures.

UNITED WE STAND, DIVIDED WE FALL
These female elephants resting in Amboseli National Park, Kenya, look relaxed and do not seem to fear attack. If danger were to threaten and there was no room or time to run away, the older animals would immediately form an outward-facing circle with the calves on the inside, shielding their vulnerable young with their own bodies.

TESTING THE WATER
The Uaso Nyiro River, in Samburu Game Reserve, Kenya, has a healthy population of Nile crocodiles. This may account for the caution being shown by this family as the matriarch strides across the shallows and the others watch with interest from the safety of the bank. Perhaps the grass really is greener on the other side, but it is up to the matriarch to find out by using her knowledge of when and where the grass grows. She has her own lifetime of experience to go on and also that learned from her mother, who learned from her mother before her.

HELPING A STICK-IN-THE-MUD
Baby elephants are vulnerable to all sorts of dangers, such as getting their feet stuck in a muddy riverbank. In the caring, sharing elephant society, however, there is always an aunt or big sister to offer a helping trunk if needed. At about five years or so, female calves begin to take on the role of nanny for their younger siblings and cousins. This not only gives the nanny practice in calf-caring, making her a better mother when she has a calf of her own, but it improves the chances of the baby surviving and not being left behind. It also gives the mother a much-needed break from the endless demands of a baby elephant.

ROCK-A-BYE BABY ELEPHANT
Adult females in a family often have babies at about the same time (such as in the rainy season). The matriarch then has to slow the pace of the herd to allow for their little steps and need for frequent naps. Herds often split up to feed for a few hours, or even a few days, and each mother-calf unit may be out of sight of the others. We now know that they keep in touch by infrasonic calls (p. 35) and get excited when they meet up again, greeting each other with sniffs and rumbles.

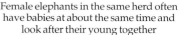

Female elephants in the same herd often have babies at about the same time and look after their young together

Ears crack like a whip against body when the head is shaken

MOTHER ON THE WARPATH
As calves grow bigger, they become more confident and are more likely to stray farther from their mother. If a calf is suddenly frightened, though, by something real or imagined, the mother will hear the alarm call and come running to protect her young. Few sights in nature are more impressive than an angry mother (who may weigh 4 tons) hurtling toward you, kicking up the dust.

DRINKING LIKE THE GROWNUPS
From the security of their mother's legs, elephant calves imitate their elders. They will gradually learn where to find food, minerals, and water throughout their herd's home range. As cows reach puberty, at about 10-15 years, they will stay in the family to give birth to the next generation. Up to four generations of females may be together in a herd, but even when the matriarch is old and weak, her position in the herd is respected.

Clash of the titans

THE LIFE OF A BULL ELEPHANT is very different from that of a cow. Elephants reach sexual maturity at about 10-15 years. At this stage, cows will mate and stay in their mother's herd to give birth. Adolescent bulls, on the other hand, are chased away as soon as they show any interest in courting females. By their mid-teens they will have left their family herd and gone off alone or joined a temporary bachelor herd. They then begin the long, slow climb up the male ladder of success, with the biggest, strongest bulls in the area at the top. These dominant bulls are the ones who are most likely to mate with estrous females (pp. 36–37). Once they have mated with a cow, however, the bulls show very little interest in their offspring. Instead, they stay out of the family herd and concentrate on keeping their status among the males in their population.

TRAIN STOPPERS
Once technology had developed powerful machines, people became fascinated by the spectacle of elephants pitted against them. This painting depicts a train held up by a herd of elephants in Assam, India.

ELEPHANT FENCING
Serious trials of strength to establish which elephant is dominant grow out of the pushing and shoving games that calves play. While female calves begin to play mother with smaller siblings, bulls continue play-fighting right through to adulthood. As their tusks grow, fencing with them becomes a major part of the competition, and the clack of ivory on ivory (which sounds just like someone playing pool) rings out in the forest or plains. A well-matched pair like the ones pictured here may grapple and prod for an hour or more, but serious wounds are rare. It seems likely that once they have established their relative strength, they will remember and behave in a way that avoids a serious fight in the future.

SUMO ELEPHANTS
With trunks wrapped in a face-embrace, these two bulls are testing for each others' weaknesses. Just as Japanese Sumo wrestlers have skilled techniques for overpowering a rival, so elephants shift their grip and angle, twist, and turn their heads – sometimes even lifting their opponent's front legs off the ground in order to drive them backward into defeat.

MALES WILL BE MALES
When male mammals meet, whether polar bears, elephants, or shrews, they usually need to sort out who is the strongest – especially when in the presence of females. As the bigger, stronger ones are more likely to win, they will pass on their genes to the next generation.

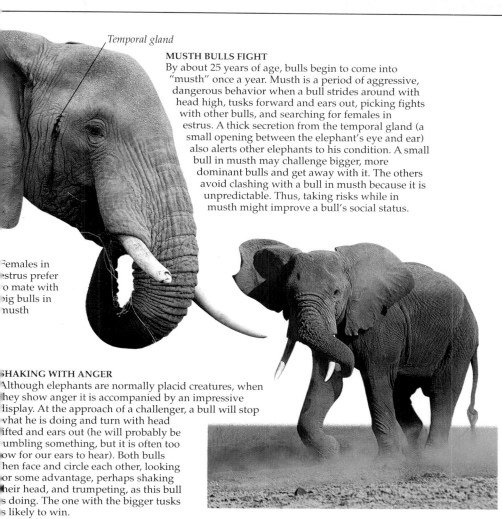

Temporal gland

MUSTH BULLS FIGHT
By about 25 years of age, bulls begin to come into "musth" once a year. Musth is a period of aggressive, dangerous behavior when a bull strides around with head high, tusks forward and ears out, picking fights with other bulls, and searching for females in estrus. A thick secretion from the temporal gland (a small opening between the elephant's eye and ear) also alerts other elephants to his condition. A small bull in musth may challenge bigger, more dominant bulls and get away with it. The others avoid clashing with a bull in musth because it is unpredictable. Thus, taking risks while in musth might improve a bull's social status.

Females in estrus prefer to mate with big bulls in musth

SHAKING WITH ANGER
Although elephants are normally placid creatures, when they show anger it is accompanied by an impressive display. At the approach of a challenger, a bull will stop what he is doing and turn with head lifted and ears out (he will probably be rumbling something, but it is often too low for our ears to hear). Both bulls then face and circle each other, looking for some advantage, perhaps shaking their head, and trumpeting, as this bull is doing. The one with the bigger tusks is likely to win.

BACHELORS HAVING A DRINK
Elephants are unusual among mammals in that they continue to grow throughout their lives, although the rate of growth slows after they reach sexual maturity. This makes it possible to estimate age in wild herds by comparing shoulder height. These drinking bulls are all different ages.

ELEPHANT FIGHTS AS A HUMAN SPORT
Miniature paintings are a popular and highly collectible form of art in India. They are designed to tell a story rather than just portray a static scene. This painting, dating from the 18th century, depicts the Mughal Royal Sports at Agra in northwest India, which included organized fights between elephants. Urged on by their riders, these fighting elephants would have fought much harder than in normal sparring but not with the intensity of a fight between bulls in musth.

The young bulls in this group probably learn a lot from old tuskers, but they do not form such strong social bonds as do the females in family herds

Keeping in touch

ELEPHANTS COMMUNICATE with each other in many ways and with all their senses. They rely less on their eyes than humans do, but visual signals are important – the position of their ears and trunk shows what mood an elephant is in. Their sense of smell can tell them something about another elephant's health or sexual condition. Touch can also be used to convey some information. But the main way an elephant communicates deliberately is, as with humans, by sound. Elephant vocalizations range from high-pitched squeaks to deep rumbles, but just how deep those rumbles are remained unknown until 1984. In that year an American scientist noticed an odd feeling while standing near the Asian elephants at a zoo in Oregon, although she could hear nothing. She took a recording with a microphone sensitive to low frequency sounds and eventually discovered that two thirds of what an elephant is saying is too low for the human ear to detect.

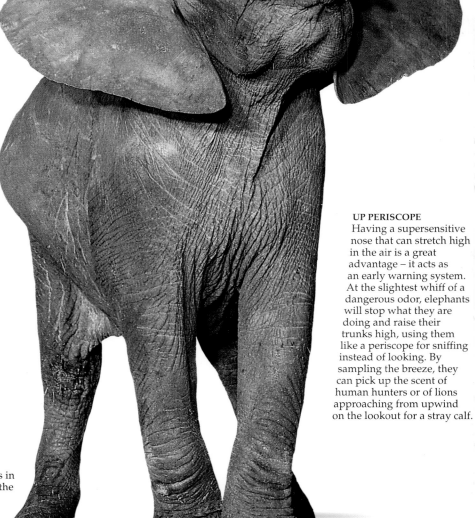

Elephants "periscope" when sniffing the air to pick up scents

TÊTE-À-TÊTE (HEAD TO HEAD)
Touch is an important way of communicating feelings in elephant society. To reassure a frightened member of the family, other elephants stand close and caress it with their trunks. To reprimand a naughty calf, a mother smacks it with her trunk. At rest, friends stand together head to head, like these Asian elephants.

UP PERISCOPE
Having a supersensitive nose that can stretch high in the air is a great advantage – it acts as an early warning system. At the slightest whiff of a dangerous odor, elephants will stop what they are doing and raise their trunks high, using them like a periscope for sniffing instead of looking. By sampling the breeze, they can pick up the scent of human hunters or of lions approaching from upwind on the lookout for a stray calf.

TRUNK GREETINGS

When elephants meet, they go through an elaborate greeting ceremony. They entwine their trunks, sniff each other's face and body, and appear to sample breath and saliva while rumbling a greeting. This allows for an exchange of touch, smell, and taste as well as sound. However, we cannot know just how much each elephant learns about the other.

SNIFF TESTS

Like dogs, elephants show a great interest in urine. When a female elephant is in estrus (in heat and ready to mate), her urine will have a slightly different odor. Male elephants will inhale this subtle scent, then curl their trunk inward to blow it over the roof of the mouth, where an array of sensors called the Jacobson's organ can detect whether the female is ready to mate.

Spreading the ears is a mild threat display

HOLDING TAILS

A young elephant needs to touch, or be touched, by its mother (or another close relative) every few seconds for reassurance. Sometimes it will take hold of her tail, just as circus elephants are trained to do.

LONG-DISTANCE TRUNK CALLS

Low frequency elephant calls (those that are too low for us to hear) may be heard by other elephants at distances of more than 5 miles (8 km). By filming the elephants' behavior while recording their inaudible calls, scientists have identified rumbles for different occasions. This bull elephant is standing still, slowly scanning the air with ears held out. Perhaps he has picked up the rumble of a distant estrous female or the challenge of another bull in musth (pp. 32–33).

A relaxed trunk means he is not really worried

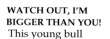

WATCH OUT, I'M BIGGER THAN YOU!

This young bull elephant is giving a mild threat display by spreading his ears to increase his apparent size. This is done to frighten another animal – in this case the photographer – who he thinks might be dangerous. He could increase the threat by "standing tall," which involves stretching up to his full height, still with ears out, and looking down his trunk with tusks raised, maybe shaking his head, flapping his ears against his body, and stepping forward as well. Such threats are a bluff and do not usually lead to an attack. But if he charges with his trunk curled up safely out of the way, his ears held flat, and his head down, it means he is about to attack.

Heavy babies

REPRODUCTION IS A RATHER SLOW AFFAIR for elephants. It takes nearly two years for a baby elephant to grow inside its mother's womb. The mother will not normally be ready to mate again until her first calf is weaned from milk, and she might give birth only once every five years or so. Because a suitable adult male may be miles away, it is important that he knows when she is in estrus (ready to mate). She attracts his attention and advertises her condition by means of both scent and sounds and, when he is close enough to see her, by the way she behaves. Baby elephants can be born at any time of the year if food is plentiful all year round. In areas where food is scarce during dry seasons, most births occur during rainy seasons. This ensures that the mother has plenty to eat while she is suckling her calf.

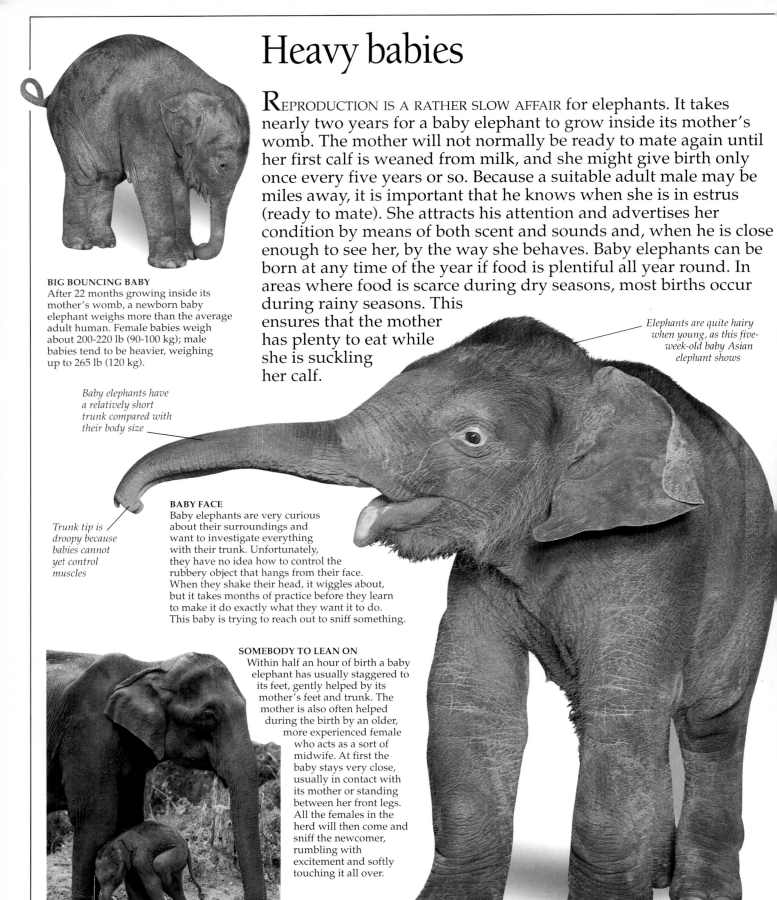

BIG BOUNCING BABY
After 22 months growing inside its mother's womb, a newborn baby elephant weighs more than the average adult human. Female babies weigh about 200-220 lb (90-100 kg); male babies tend to be heavier, weighing up to 265 lb (120 kg).

Baby elephants have a relatively short trunk compared with their body size

Elephants are quite hairy when young, as this five-week-old baby Asian elephant shows

Trunk tip is droopy because babies cannot yet control muscles

BABY FACE
Baby elephants are very curious about their surroundings and want to investigate everything with their trunk. Unfortunately, they have no idea how to control the rubbery object that hangs from their face. When they shake their head, it wiggles about, but it takes months of practice before they learn to make it do exactly what they want it to do. This baby is trying to reach out to sniff something.

SOMEBODY TO LEAN ON
Within half an hour of birth a baby elephant has usually staggered to its feet, gently helped by its mother's feet and trunk. The mother is also often helped during the birth by an older, more experienced female who acts as a sort of midwife. At first the baby stays very close, usually in contact with its mother or standing between her front legs. All the females in the herd will then come and sniff the newcomer, rumbling with excitement and softly touching it all over.

A one-day-old Asian baby leans on its mother for comfort

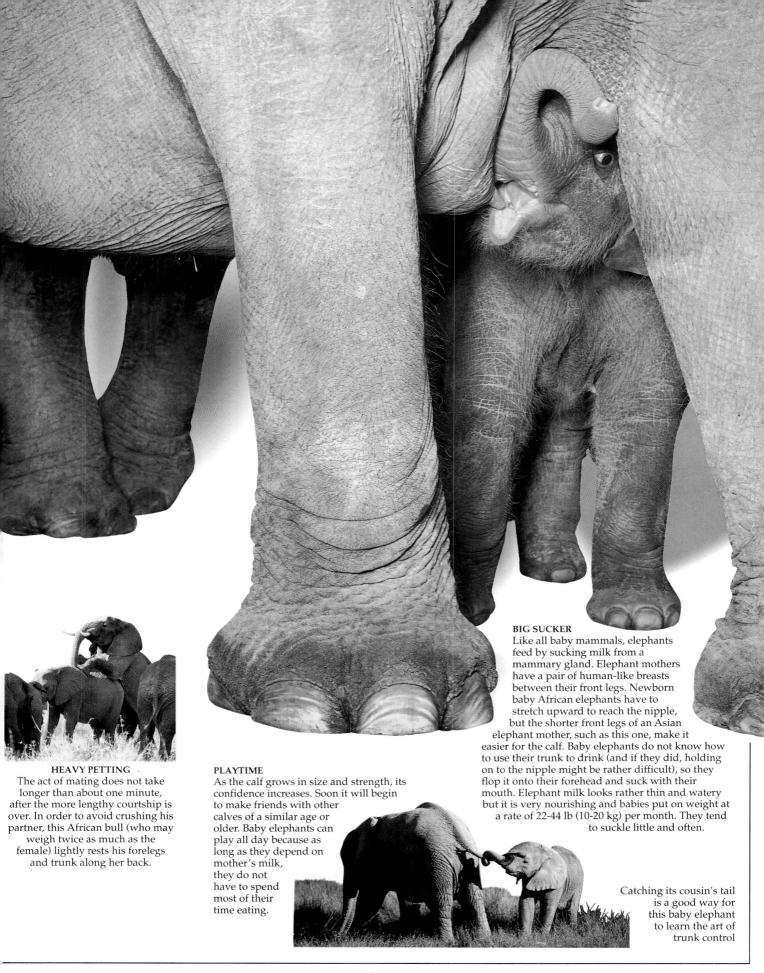

BIG SUCKER
Like all baby mammals, elephants feed by sucking milk from a mammary gland. Elephant mothers have a pair of human-like breasts between their front legs. Newborn baby African elephants have to stretch upward to reach the nipple, but the shorter front legs of an Asian elephant mother, such as this one, make it easier for the calf. Baby elephants do not know how to use their trunk to drink (and if they did, holding on to the nipple might be rather difficult), so they flop it onto their forehead and suck with their mouth. Elephant milk looks rather thin and watery but it is very nourishing and babies put on weight at a rate of 22-44 lb (10-20 kg) per month. They tend to suckle little and often.

HEAVY PETTING
The act of mating does not take longer than about one minute, after the more lengthy courtship is over. In order to avoid crushing his partner, this African bull (who may weigh twice as much as the female) lightly rests his forelegs and trunk along her back.

PLAYTIME
As the calf grows in size and strength, its confidence increases. Soon it will begin to make friends with other calves of a similar age or older. Baby elephants can play all day because as long as they depend on mother's milk, they do not have to spend most of their time eating.

Catching its cousin's tail is a good way for this baby elephant to learn the art of trunk control

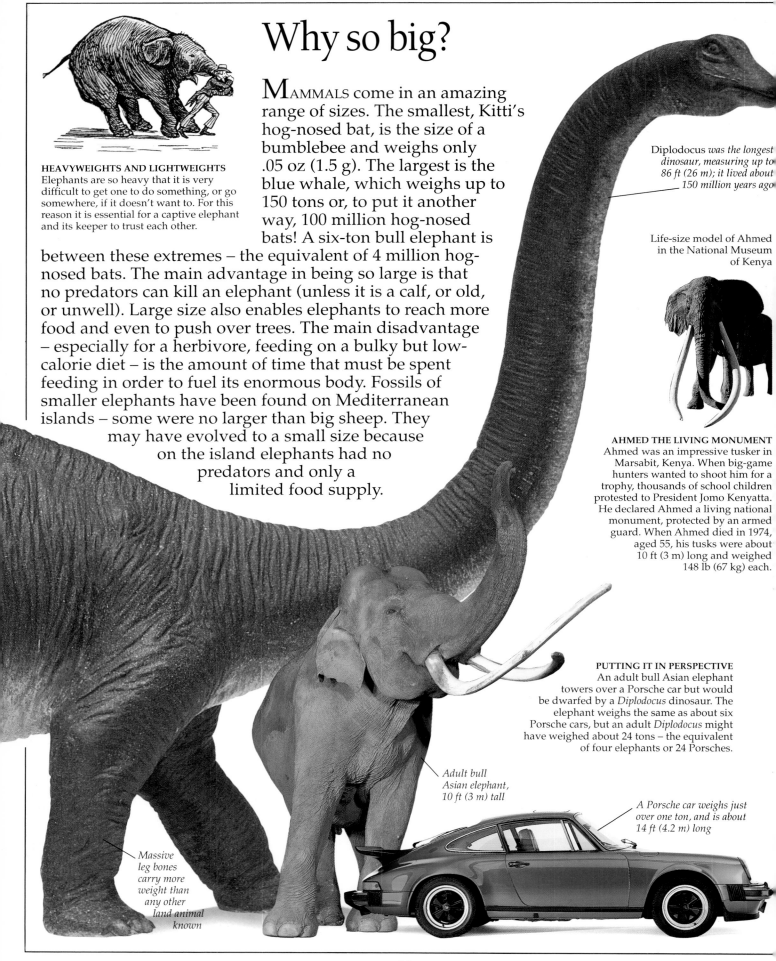

Why so big?

MAMMALS come in an amazing range of sizes. The smallest, Kitti's hog-nosed bat, is the size of a bumblebee and weighs only .05 oz (1.5 g). The largest is the blue whale, which weighs up to 150 tons or, to put it another way, 100 million hog-nosed bats! A six-ton bull elephant is between these extremes – the equivalent of 4 million hog-nosed bats. The main advantage in being so large is that no predators can kill an elephant (unless it is a calf, or old, or unwell). Large size also enables elephants to reach more food and even to push over trees. The main disadvantage – especially for a herbivore, feeding on a bulky but low-calorie diet – is the amount of time that must be spent feeding in order to fuel its enormous body. Fossils of smaller elephants have been found on Mediterranean islands – some were no larger than big sheep. They may have evolved to a small size because on the island elephants had no predators and only a limited food supply.

HEAVYWEIGHTS AND LIGHTWEIGHTS
Elephants are so heavy that it is very difficult to get one to do something, or go somewhere, if it doesn't want to. For this reason it is essential for a captive elephant and its keeper to trust each other.

Diplodocus was the longest dinosaur, measuring up to 86 ft (26 m); it lived about 150 million years ago

Life-size model of Ahmed in the National Museum of Kenya

AHMED THE LIVING MONUMENT
Ahmed was an impressive tusker in Marsabit, Kenya. When big-game hunters wanted to shoot him for a trophy, thousands of school children protested to President Jomo Kenyatta. He declared Ahmed a living national monument, protected by an armed guard. When Ahmed died in 1974, aged 55, his tusks were about 10 ft (3 m) long and weighed 148 lb (67 kg) each.

PUTTING IT IN PERSPECTIVE
An adult bull Asian elephant towers over a Porsche car but would be dwarfed by a *Diplodocus* dinosaur. The elephant weighs the same as about six Porsche cars, but an adult *Diplodocus* might have weighed about 24 tons – the equivalent of four elephants or 24 Porsches.

Adult bull Asian elephant, 10 ft (3 m) tall

A Porsche car weighs just over one ton, and is about 14 ft (4.2 m) long

Massive leg bones carry more weight than any other land animal known

NOT MUCH SKIN ON AN ELEPHANT

Small animals, such as mice, have trouble keeping warm in cold weather, and elephants have a problem keeping cool in hot weather (p. 28–29). One way to understand this is to compare how much skin (surface area) each animal has to how much muscle, bones, and organs (volume) it has. This is called the "surface area to volume ratio" (SA:V). It is easier to figure out if we simplify the animal's shape. For example, a cube-shaped mouse may have a ratio of 1:0.5, which means one square inch of mouse-skin has to lose heat from only half a cubic inch of mouse-muscle. For a cube-shaped elephant the ratio may be 1:33, so one square inch of elephant-skin loses heat from 33 cubic inches of elephant-muscle. For a zebra the ratio may be in-between, about 1:17.

Cubed zebra

Cubed mouse

Cubed elephant

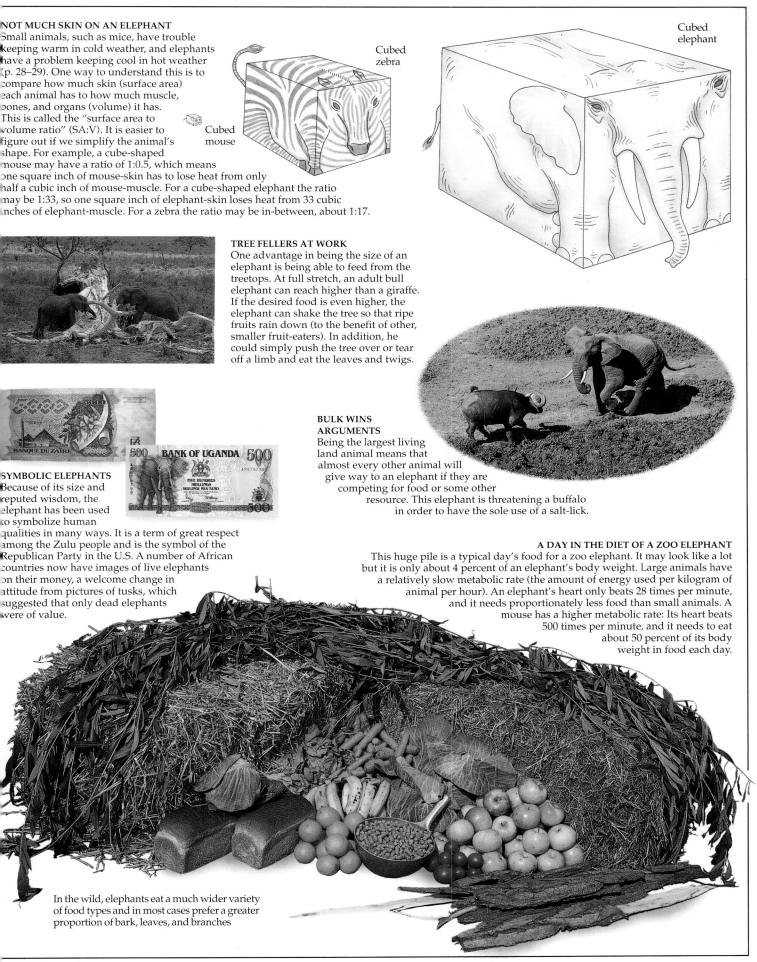

TREE FELLERS AT WORK

One advantage in being the size of an elephant is being able to feed from the treetops. At full stretch, an adult bull elephant can reach higher than a giraffe. If the desired food is even higher, the elephant can shake the tree so that ripe fruits rain down (to the benefit of other, smaller fruit-eaters). In addition, he could simply push the tree over or tear off a limb and eat the leaves and twigs.

SYMBOLIC ELEPHANTS

Because of its size and reputed wisdom, the elephant has been used to symbolize human qualities in many ways. It is a term of great respect among the Zulu people and is the symbol of the Republican Party in the U.S. A number of African countries now have images of live elephants on their money, a welcome change in attitude from pictures of tusks, which suggested that only dead elephants were of value.

BANQUE DU ZAÏRE 5000

BANK OF UGANDA 500

BULK WINS ARGUMENTS

Being the largest living land animal means that almost every other animal will give way to an elephant if they are competing for food or some other resource. This elephant is threatening a buffalo in order to have the sole use of a salt-lick.

A DAY IN THE DIET OF A ZOO ELEPHANT

This huge pile is a typical day's food for a zoo elephant. It may look like a lot but it is only about 4 percent of an elephant's body weight. Large animals have a relatively slow metabolic rate (the amount of energy used per kilogram of animal per hour). An elephant's heart only beats 28 times per minute, and it needs proportionately less food than small animals. A mouse has a higher metabolic rate: Its heart beats 500 times per minute, and it needs to eat about 50 percent of its body weight in food each day.

In the wild, elephants eat a much wider variety of food types and in most cases prefer a greater proportion of bark, leaves, and branches

Big brains too

THE SAYING "AN ELEPHANT NEVER FORGETS" is close to the truth. Elephants do have a remarkable memory. In the wild, elephants appear to remember for years their relationships with dozens, perhaps hundreds, of other elephants, some of whom they may see only occasionally. The advantages of a good memory may explain why they have evolved such a large brain. An adult bull elephant has the largest brain of any land animal that has ever lived, measuring 6,600 cubic centimeters (cc). Adult human brains average only 1,350 cc, but it is important to relate brain size to body size. A human brain is about 2 percent of the total body weight, whereas an elephant's brain is only about 0.1 percent of its body weight.

AT THE BALLET
The intelligent elephant has long been a favorite subject in stories and cartoons. Characters are often wise, are dressed in clothes, have the power of human speech, and are cultured, as in this 19th-century print.

Elephant mothers shade their sleeping babies from the sun's rays

SHADOWY BABY-SITTER
Elephants have a keen awareness and understanding of their surroundings and an ability to reason and plan ahead. These female African elephants, for example, are casting their shadow over their sleeping babies to keep them cool. As the sun moves across the sky, the mothers move every so often to make sure that their shadow stays over the calf on the ground.

ELEANOR HELPS HERSELF
Eleanor is a Kenyan elephant who was orphaned at an early age. She was reared by Daphne Sheldrick, a foster mother to animals. Eleanor grew up in a mixed-species family that included buffaloes, rhinos, and zebras. They became famous as the Orphans of Tsavo. Eleanor learned how to open the latch on the barn where food was kept and how to turn on faucets. Nowadays Eleanor spends most of her time with wild elephants, but she often visits her human "matriarch" and voluntarily helps to reintroduce other elephant orphans to a life in the wild.

Elephants, like humans and apes, make and use tools (such as a fly-swatter), so opening a door latch is easy

Once inside, Eleanor's trunk probes for stores of oats and hay

40

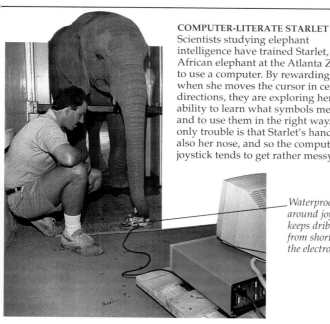

COMPUTER-LITERATE STARLET

Scientists studying elephant intelligence have trained Starlet, an African elephant at the Atlanta Zoo, to use a computer. By rewarding her when she moves the cursor in certain directions, they are exploring her ability to learn what symbols mean and to use them in the right way. The only trouble is that Starlet's hand is also her nose, and so the computer joystick tends to get rather messy!

Waterproof tape around joystick keeps dribbles from shorting the electronics

WORK OF ART

An art critic might describe this as a bold, exciting, uninhibited piece of modern art. But can it be art if it is painted by an elephant? Some people apparently think so, because framed paintings such as this one by Starlet can fetch hundreds of dollars at auctions to raise funds for zoos.

ELEPHANT DEXTERITY

Working elephants quickly become adept at lifting, moving, and stacking heavy logs – or whatever tasks they are set. Once they get to know the job they are doing, they will work with few commands, and have been known to point out mistakes made by their *mahout* (driver). A World War II officer in Burma who saw them at work wrote "the trained elephant was no mere transport animal, but indeed a skilled sapper" (a sapper is a soldier in the Royal Engineers).

ELEPHANT PAINTING

Elephants in captivity have sometimes been seen to pick up a stick or stone and doodle a pattern on the floor of their enclosure. Whether or not this shows an artistic ability is unclear, but some zoos have begun to give their elephants painting sessions. Here Starlet is using a house painting brush with the handle sawn off, holding it in her "trunk-fingers".

Brush held between "trunk fingers"

MOURNING THE DEAD

Elephants have a strange fascination with their dead. When one dies, others will sometimes cover the body with branches, grass, and soil. If a herd comes across a long-dead elephant, the members will feel and sniff the remains, pick up and scatter bones, draw the tusks from the skull, and sometimes smash them. Even when no sign is left, they may pause where a relative died, as if recalling the lost family member.

HELPING THE SICK

If an elephant is sick or injured, any family members present will rush to assist. Hunters have described how two elephants will stand on either side of a wounded comrade to hold it up and help it shuffle away. Mothers will use their trunk and forefoot to try to rouse a sick calf or will even carry a weak baby across their tusks.

Salt-mining elephants

ALL ANIMALS – including the human animal – need salt and will go to great lengths to get enough. It is because of this hunger for salt, called salt appetite, that food tastes good with salt sprinkled on it. Without salt our bodies would not work, though too much salt is bad for our health. Animals seem to know when they have had enough salt, but if the food they eat is low in salt they will start to look for it. Elephants, for example, will sample all sorts of substances for their salt content – even rocks and soil. If they find something that satisfies their craving for salt, they eat it and remember where they found it, for future use. This is how outcrops of mineral-rich rock become a salt-lick for the local animals. The eating of rocks and soil is called geophagy. The rock might not taste salty to us because instead of table salt (sodium chloride), which we are used to, it might contain other salts that taste different.

Elephants push with their bodies to dig up earth with their tusks

BIG DIGGERS
Although they visit salt-licks regularly, salt-hungry elephants cannot lick like other animals. Their tongues are not long enough to reach around the trunk and tusks. Soil or rock must be dug up with the point of a tusk and then picked up by the trunk tip and placed into the mouth, where it is ground up between the massive molars and swallowed. Salt-digging elephants appear to be doing a head stand as they push with their bodies to drive their tusks deep into the ground to loosen the earth. Clod after clod of salty earth may be eaten at a rate of about 50 lb (23 kg) in one hour.

STRIPED LICKERS
Zebras lick and nibble the salty ground to make up for a lack of salt in their food plants. Normally, only plant-eating animals – herbivores – need to search for extra salt. If a leopard or a pack of hyenas visits a salt-lick, it is to prey upon one of the lickers. Its prey has already made up for the lack of salt, and so the predator gets its meat ready-salted.

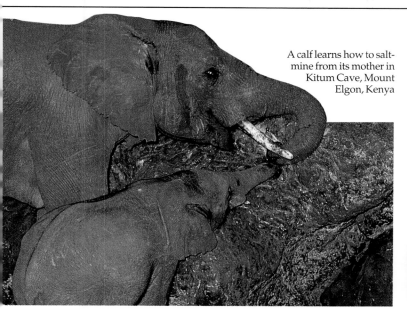

A calf learns how to salt-mine from its mother in Kitum Cave, Mount Elgon, Kenya

IVORY CHISELS

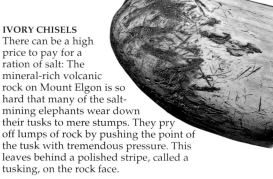

There can be a high price to pay for a ration of salt: The mineral-rich volcanic rock on Mount Elgon is so hard that many of the salt-mining elephants wear down their tusks to mere stumps. They pry off lumps of rock by pushing the point of the tusk with tremendous pressure. This leaves behind a polished stripe, called a tusking, on the rock face.

ELEPHANT-CAVE CULTURE

Baby elephants do not need extra salt so long as their mothers suckle them, but as they are weaned they must learn from their mothers to find salt. For an elephant living in the forests of Mount Elgon, an extinct volcano in Kenya, this means following its mother into totally dark caves and mining rock deep underground. The Elgon elephants are unique in their use of these subterranean salt-licks. Kitum Cave (above and right) extends 525 ft (160 m) into the mountainside. Whole families disappear into the cave mouth, stretching their trunks out to feel the way and walking trunk to tail in single file around the huge rocks and deep, dangerous crevasses that block their path.

SALT ROCK *below*
The rock that attracts elephants and other animals to the Elgon caves is called volcanic agglomerate. It is made up of old ash thrown out by the volcano about 10 million years ago. The ash contains Glauber's salt (sodium sulfate).

Calcite

CRUNCHING UP CRYSTALS *left*

The rock contains various crystals in addition to the salts the cave elephants are seeking. The white ones here are calcite, and the glassy needles are natrolite. It may be that eating natrolite is also good for the animals visiting the cave. It belongs to a family of minerals called zeolites – when ground up and added to farm-animal feeds, they act as a general tonic to improve the animals' health.

Natrolite

Particle of rock

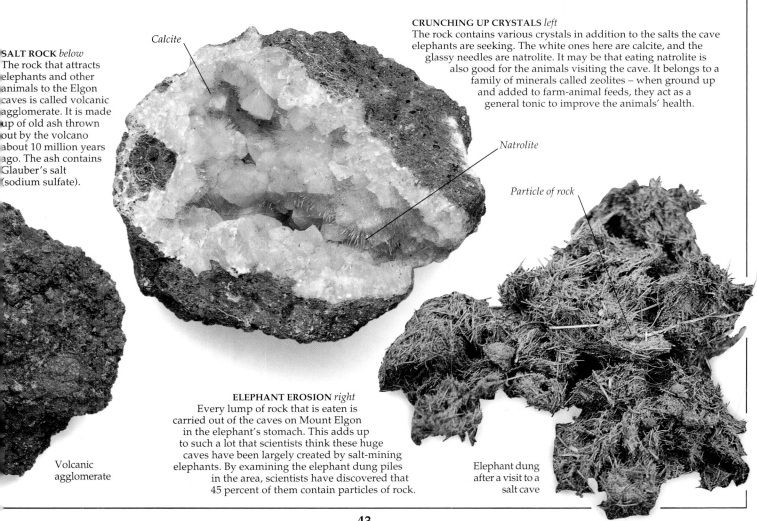

Volcanic agglomerate

ELEPHANT EROSION *right*

Every lump of rock that is eaten is carried out of the caves on Mount Elgon in the elephant's stomach. This adds up to such a lot that scientists think these huge caves have been largely created by salt-mining elephants. By examining the elephant dung piles in the area, scientists have discovered that 45 percent of them contain particles of rock.

Elephant dung after a visit to a salt cave

Harnessing nature's bulldozer

WORKING ELEPHANTS have long been widespread in Asia, although it is not known whether the first elephants to be captured and trained were African or Asian. The earliest hint of their domestication is found in carved seals from the Indus Valley civilization of 1,500 B.C. The North African general Hannibal (p. 46) used both Asian and African elephants in his campaigns. However, after the North African elephants were wiped out during the Roman Empire, no training of African elephants is known to have taken place until the late 19th century when the Belgians began a domestication scheme in the Congo, which continues to this day in what is now Zaire. During the British rule in India, Burma (now Myanmar), and Siam (now Thailand), large-scale logging was developed by using thousands of Asian elephants to fell teak trees in the forested hills.

TRUNK COIL
Small logs are easily carried in the powerful coil of the trunk tip.

TRUNK ROLL
Elephants do not make good pack animals because their backs will not take much more than half a ton (about 500 kg). But when it comes to lifting, pushing, and hauling weights, they are unbeatable. Modern machines may be more powerful, but they cannot work in the rough terrain in which an elephant excels. The elephant's role in the timber industry has declined with the advent of machines, but in Myanmar, elephants still extract 50 percent of teak trees harvested – without destroying the rest of the forest. Some countries are returning to elephant power, and new training camps have been established to train young elephants.

One elephant can haul a log weighing more than four tons; sometimes two elephants are harnessed together to pull even bigger logs

FORK-LIFT TUSKER
Despite the problems associated with musth (pp. 32–33), bulls are used as working elephants as well as cows. In logging operations, bulls are preferred because they are not only bigger and stronger but their tusks provide an extra carrying device. A working tusker (bull with tusks) soon learns to slide his tusks under a load, like a fork-lift truck. Then, using his trunk to steady the load, the elephant moves it to wherever the rider directs.

GOLDEN GOAD
Trained elephants are controlled by words of command and by signals from the rider's toes moving behind the elephant's ears. The driver (*mahout* in India, *oozie* in Myanmar) will also carry a spiked stick, or *ankus*, but the sharp points are seldom used.

This ceremonial Indian *ankus*, with diamonds set in enamel, was made c. 1870

AFRICAN SAFARI
Tourists can now take elephant-back safaris in Africa as well as Asia. Abu, the bull elephant shown here, was brought from a safari park in the U.S. and shipped to Botswana. He carries visitors through the swamps of the Okavango Delta on an unforgettable ride, living proof that those who say the African elephant cannot be trained are wrong. Other safari operators are now following this example elsewhere in Africa.

ELEPHANT PRESS-GANG
Unlike any other working animal, the elephant has never been domesticated by breeding. Captive births are rare, so each new generation of elephants must be captured from the wild, subdued, and trained. New elephants were often captured in a *keddah*, a huge funnel-shaped corral into which wild elephants were driven. A brave handler would then dart in and slip a rope around the selected elephant's leg while trained elephants calmed the frightened newcomer. Nowadays wild elephants can be immobilized with a dart-gun and then tied and transported to the training camp. This is more humane and carries less risk of injury to either human or elephant.

Once they get used to a job, elephants can do it with very little guidance from their human trainer

WORK FOR EX-TIMBER ELEPHANTS
The growth in wildlife tourism has provided a boost to the local economy and jobs for both humans and elephants in and around many national parks in Asia. Watching tigers, deer, or even wild elephants while riding on elephant-back is an experience not to be forgotten – particularly when your elephant decides to cross a deep river, as here in Kaziranga National Park, India.

Elephants as tanks

MILITARY COMMANDERS have used elephants to help conquer their enemies since before the time of Alexander the Great. And what could be more terrifying to a simple foot soldier than his first glimpse of a moving, trumpeting mountain of muscle, topped by enemy archers firing down at him? War elephants were valued as much for their psychological effect as for their ability to trample or gore the enemy. But elephants are not usually aggressive animals, and enemy commanders soon realized that once injured or badly frightened, a terrified elephant running away would trample friend and foe alike. For this reason, elephants gradually lost favor in the front line. Even today, however, they are sometimes used in jungle warfare – for moving men or heavy loads where machines cannot operate.

ARMOR-PLATED ELEPHANT
Made in India around 1600, this suit of elephant armor is the only known example of its kind. When complete, it consisted of 8,439 overlapping metal plates linked with chain mail and sewn onto a cloth. The total weight is 350 lb (159 kg). It was also equipped with tusk-swords. It was acquired by Lady Clive, wife of the governor of Madras. She brought it home to England in 1801.

The chanfron protected the head. This one weighs 60 lb (27 kg)

Hannibal is said to have crossed the Rhone River with his elephants on rafts

ALPINE SURPRISE
Hannibal (247-183 B.C.) and his war elephants came close to bringing the Roman Empire to an end. Hannibal was a young general from the North African city Carthage, which was at war with Rome. He won fame by attacking Italy from the north. In 218 B.C., he led 40,000 men and 38 elephants via Spain and over the French Alpine passes and took the Romans by surprise. Although outnumbered, Hannibal won several battles but stopped short of attacking Rome itself

ELEPHANT AND CASTLE
This illustration from a 13th-century English manuscript shows a castle-like howdah strapped to an elephant's back. Julius Caesar is reported to have used such a device while invading Britain in 54 B.C. The sight of one war elephant (the first elephant to set foot in Britain in 10,000 years) was enough to send the Britons, with their horses and chariots, running, thus allowing the Roman army to cross the Thames River.

REGENCY ELEPHANTS
The theme of the "elephant and castle" is found in many different forms, ranging from these early 19th-century Regency candle-holders to English pub signs and a London Underground (subway) station. The elephant is portrayed wearing a castle on its back from which soldiers could fight the enemy.

HERALDIC ELEPHANTS
As well as having their own armor, elephants sometimes appear on armorial crests such as this one for Lord Oliphant. It shows two elephants standing on their back legs supporting the Oliphant shield.

AIRCRAFT CARRIER
During World War II, elephants played many important roles in the Allied war effort, from hauling planes at a British Fleet Air Arm base near the Indian Ocean (right) to helping to build hundreds of bridges, including the famous bridge over the River Kwai in Thailand.

THE ORIGINAL ALL-TERRAIN VEHICLE
As well as being a useful vehicle from which humans could kill other humans, elephants were used as mobile hunting platforms for the pursuit of other animals. They could push through the thickest bushes, ford rivers, and climb hills, while the hunters sat in luxury with no risk of injury. This painting shows an Indian dignitary hunting boars from the back of an elephant in 1855.

JUNGLE PATROL
Imagine a military vehicle that can move silently and with equal ease through forested hills or along main roads; this amazing vehicle gives a high vantage point for reconnaissance patrols, but leaves no tire tracks; most astonishing of all, it runs on vegetation and can even refuel itself as it goes along. These are among the reasons why elephants are still used in certain military campaigns today. They particularly lend themselves to guerrilla warfare in jungles and have been used in many of the recent wars in Southeast Asia.

Khmer soldiers patrol on elephant-back in Cambodia

TIGER HUNTING
Of all the species hunted from elephant-back, tigers carried the greatest prestige. This scene from the British Raj (when Britain ruled India) in 1807 was typical of the kind of outing organized by aristocrats and colonial officers.

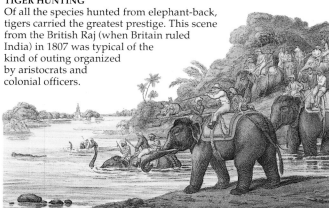

Elephants as gods

IN MANY HUMAN CULTURES, things that are bigger or more powerful than people have been worshipped as gods. Temples have been dedicated to anything from the sun and the moon to mythological monsters. It is hardly surprising, therefore, to find that elephants feature a great deal in several religions. In some cases the elephant itself is a god, in others the god or prophet rides on an elephant, and in the best known example, Ganesha the Hindu god has the head of an elephant. Buddhists have a number of beliefs about elephants. In the *Jakatas* (stories about Buddha's previous lives on Earth) the Great Being is born in the body of an elephant, rides on an elephant, and in one story is born into an elephant trainer's family. Some Buddhists think that to touch an elephant helps to achieve enlightenment, and so elephants are often kept in Buddhist monasteries.

WHITE ELEPHANT STALL
There is no such thing as a totally white elephant, but for centuries any albino or pale wild elephant would be captured and brought to the court of the king of Siam (now Thailand). There, pale elephants were worshipped and treated as the king's equal. Their stall was like a palace. They were never ridden. Even the king was considered unworthy of riding on a white elephant.

FLYING ELEPHANTS GROUNDED
A widespread Indian folk tale tells of a distant time when elephants roamed everywhere, in the sky as well as on Earth. One day an old hermit was meditating beneath a huge banyan tree when a rowdy flock of elephants began crashing about in the branches above him. He finally lost his temper when a branch fell on him and used his special powers of thought to take away their wings. From that time on, no elephant has ever grown wings.

DECORATED ELEPHANTS
Elephant decoration has become an art form in many Asian countries, and colorful models are frequently kept in people's houses for good luck. As well as having their skin painted (p. 6) and being dressed in decorative harnesses and straps, some elephants today take part in processions with strings of light bulbs draped over their bodies.

BEARING THE TOOTH
Every year on Perahera Day in Kandy, Sri Lanka, a religious relic said to contain an actual tooth of Buddha is the focus of a huge parade with 100 decorated elephants. The relic is carried by the biggest elephant with the most impressive tusks.

Most statues of Ganesha have four arms. They can have up to 16 arms, each holding a symbolic object such as a lotus flower, a hatchet to cut off one tusk, or the end of the broken tusk which Ganesha is said to have used to write the *Mahabharata* (a sacred text).

Club, used for clearing obstacles

Noose, used as a weapon to bind enemies

This hand may be holding the tip of a tusk

Conch shell, used as a wind instrument

Ganesha enjoyed food and is always pictured with a potbelly

GANESHA THE COLORFUL
All over India, hundreds of colorful statues of Ganesha are dropped into the sea and in rivers every year at the end of a ten-day festival that celebrates Ganesha's birth.

ROCK SOLID ELEPHANT
The widespread worship of elephants in Asia means that almost every temple or important building has elephant statues and friezes. This whole temple (left), as well as the elephant shown, was carved out of solid rock in the 7th century at Mamallapuram, India, where it still stands today.

EVERY HOME SHOULD HAVE ONE
Ganesha (or Ganesa) is the popular Hindu god of students and teachers, the remover of obstacles and bringer of good fortune. Hindu scriptures give several versions of how Ganesha lost his human head. One of these relates that it was due to his father Shiva's terrible temper. One day, Ganesha prevented Shiva from entering the chambers of his mother Parvati because she was bathing. Shiva was so angry that he struck off Ganesha's head. Parvati insisted that their son be saved, and Shiva gave him the head of the first animal that passed by, which turned out to be an elephant. People pray to Ganesha for help when setting out on a journey or business enterprise or when taking exams.

Elephant entertainers

Just LOOKING AT AN ELEPHANT is entertaining. An elephant housed in a zoo is sure to draw a crowd. But elephants have been trained to do many things to amuse people, from complex dance routines to thrilling balancing acts. Their gentle nature and great intelligence make elephants ideal subjects for animal trainers. By building on natural behavior patterns, elephant trainers have persuaded their elephants to walk on their back legs, to balance on a huge ball, and even to do one-handed "handstands" – a trick that can damage an adult elephant because it is too heavy. But many people now question whether it is right to make an intelligent social mammal do such things for our enjoyment. Now that elephants are endangered, should we not concentrate on breeding them?

ELEPHANTS AT THE RACES
Elephants are used in different parts of the world for a variety of competitive sports. There is elephant polo, elephant soccer, elephant tug-of-war, and elephant racing, shown here in Germany.

JUMBO'S NAME LIVES ON
The most famous elephant was Jumbo, a huge bull African who came to the London Zoo in 1865. He gave rides to children for 17 years, then became a circus star in the U.S. Jumbo's name is now a word for "extra large."

TRICKS OF THE TRADE
This Asian elephant, in an English zoo, will do a headstand like this (right) on command. Although she is seldom asked to do so, she remembers it from her early years spent in a circus. This is, however, a natural action that she has been trained to do. In the wild, elephants adopt this position when digging for mineral-rich soil (p. 42). The trick is not cruel in itself, but in order to perform it for a circus audience, the elephant would have had to spend most of her time, day and night, chained to the floor of a trailer or to wooden boards in a drafty tent.

BIG-EARS RESCUES TARZAN

In the novels of Edgar Rice Burroughs, Tarzan was brought up by a female ape in Africa, where he befriended Tantor the elephant. But when films of the novels were first made, only Asian elephants were available. Hollywood enterprise solved the problem with a simple conversion kit : stick-on African ears!

ELEPHANTS FOR CHILDREN

Many children discover that "E is for Elephant" when learning their alphabet. From then on, children's books and films are full of elephants such as Dumbo, Babar, Nellie, and the Heffalump in Winnie the Pooh (right).

In this scene from the movie *Tarzan Escapes*, Tarzan is about to be rescued by an "African" elephant

UNDER THE BIG TOP

Elephants have been a part of the circus since circuses began in the days of the Roman Empire. Generations of children have marveled at their size, strength, and skills. But the more people learn about the complexity of elephant behavior in the wild and the rich social life of the herd, the more uncomfortable they feel with the elephant's role in the circus, where not all its biological and social needs can be met.

Elephant trainers point out that performing tricks is good exercise and mental stimulation for elephants, relieving the boredom of life in captivity

GETTING THE POINT

Elephants are 60-100 times heavier than humans, so the keeper must always be in control when training an elephant. Almost all elephant keepers carry a stout stick with two metal points at the end, one curved and one straight. The stick is called an *ankus*, or goad, and is used to prompt the elephant into moving or stopping as required. The good trainer prods lightly to guide the elephant and never draws blood.

THE IMPOSSIBLE BABY

Baby Motty won world fame as soon as he was born in 1977 at the Chester Zoo in England. His mother was an Asian elephant and his father an African. Motty's parents were not only of different species but of different genera – their genetic lines were as far apart as those of a chimp and a gorilla. Motty, the impossible hybrid, died at 10 days of age after making zoological history.

Elephants in art

I MAGES OF ELEPHANTS can be found around the world, in almost every branch of art. From the creators of the earliest known cave paintings to 20th-century practitioners of modern art, artists have tried to capture their impressions of elephantine size and strength. Sculptors have created elephants of all sizes from every kind of material imaginable, including ivory – the subjects' own front teeth. In Asia, because of the domestication of elephants, even very early works are reasonably accurate representations. In Europe, on the other hand, the comical paws and trumpet-like trunks of early elephant illustrations suggest that the artists were working from second-hand descriptions of an animal they had never seen. Nowadays, African elephants are one of the most popular species for wildlife artists to depict, and huge sums of money have been raised for conservation by the sale of such works of art.

ROCK ARTISTS
Some people speculate that art originated when Stone Age hunters scratched the shape of their prey animals onto cave walls or fragments of bone, perhaps to improve the chances of a successful hunt. This may be why San ("Bushmen") in Namibia left this elephant rock carving at Twyfelfontein.

UNBELIEVABLE CARGO
Elephants are so familiar to people today that it is difficult to imagine the disbelief which greeted them when travellers first brought them to countries where they had never been seen. This painting shows the 13th-century explorer Marco Polo arriving at the Gulf of Persia with elephants and camels.

SILK ELEPHANT
Hiroshi Yoshida (1876-1950) was the last of the traditional Japanese woodblock printmakers. He traveled widely through Asia and made his beautiful elephant print while in India. Despite his eye for detail, he appears to have somewhat exaggerated its size.

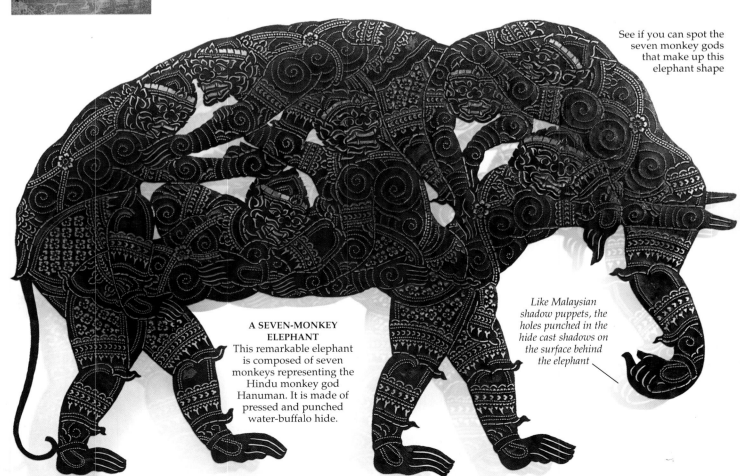

See if you can spot the seven monkey gods that make up this elephant shape

A SEVEN-MONKEY ELEPHANT
This remarkable elephant is composed of seven monkeys representing the Hindu monkey god Hanuman. It is made of pressed and punched water-buffalo hide.

Like Malaysian shadow puppets, the holes punched in the hide cast shadows on the surface behind the elephant

REMBRANDT'S ELEPHANT
At a time when natural history illustrators were drawing hopelessly inaccurate elephants, the Dutch artist Rembrandt (1606-1669) managed to capture the essence of the Asian species in this simple charcoal drawing. Rembrandt is best known for his portraits, but he also made thousands of sketches of many subjects, including this, one of the first elephants seen in Amsterdam.

ELEPHANT ON THE ROOF
In China, important buildings, such as temples and "clan halls" (village meeting places), often have decorative roof tiles on the corners, even today. This example probably originated in Taiwan.

WIRE ELEPHANT
Ceremonial elephants play an important role in many Hindu festivals. They are decorated with bejeweled gold faceplates and carry an ornate *howdah*, or platform, topped by colorful ceremonial umbrellas called *kudas*. This model is made out of brass wire, coiled and soldered into shape and filled with black clay.

NAGASAKI PRINT
A 16th-century woodblock print depicting one of the first elephants ever seen in Japan. It is rare for such prints to have text alongside, but the artist felt it was necessary to explain what elephants were to an audience who knew nothing of them.

Bronze figure sits here

ELEPHANT BELL
This Asian brass elephant is a 19th-century table bell, probably used to call for servants. The bell is in the back of the head, and it rings when the tusks (made of imitation ivory) are pressed down.

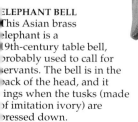

INCENSE ELEPHANT
This Chinese bronze antique has a seated figure that lifts off to reveal a hollow elephant filled with sand. Joss sticks can be stuck into the sand and burned during religious ceremonies.

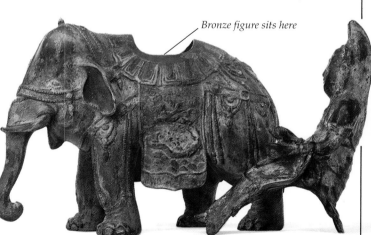

White gold

IVORY HAS BEEN USED since people first began making primitive tools. Right up until the invention of plastics, ivory was carved into everything from musical instruments and knife handles to electrical insulators and billiard balls. Artists have been attracted to ivory for almost as long: some of the earliest known works of art are rotund ivory figurines called Aurignacian Venuses, which were carved in mammoth ivory some 27,000 years ago. Since then, the demand for ivory has grown steadily. Ivory is certainly a beautiful substance – smooth and cool to the touch, easily carved but durable. If the raw material was collected from elephants that had died of old age, when their tusks had reached their maximum size, who could object? Sadly, however, the truth is that more blood – both human and elephant – has been spilled in the quest for this "white gold" than for any other raw material.

Egyptian ivory clappers from 1430 B.C.

IVORY TRIBUTE
Ivory was highly valued as long ago as the 9th century B.C. This detail from an obelisk shows men carrying tusks as a tribute to an Assyrian king.

SLAVE LABOR
Before roads and railways, transporting ivory from the interior of Africa was a problem. Some traders captured villages, stole their ivory, and forced the inhabitants to carry the tusks to the coast. Then they sold their captives into slavery.

Some ivory traders exchanged beads and cloth for tusks then hired porters to carry them

IVORY IN CHURCH
Among the works of art to be found in churches are many ivory carvings. This is half of an ivory diptych (a pair of pictures hinged together) which dates from A.D. 400. It shows an important man in an elephant-drawn funeral carriage and the same man being taken up to heaven.

One leaf of an ivory diptych

IVORY TO SIT UPON
The use of solid ivory for large items, such as furniture, was reserved for royalty: King Solomon is said to have sat upon an ivory throne, and Queen Victoria was given one in 1851. Ivory was more commonly used as a thin veneer, often inlaid with wood to produce beautiful polished patterns. Indian craftworkers were renowned for this work. This revolving armchair from Vizagaptam, eastern India, dates from the early 18th century.

How many families of elephants died to keep this billiard-ball maker in business?

IVORY BALLS
During the 19th and early 20th centuries, the increasing popularity of pool and billiards created a heavy demand for ivory to be made into balls for these games. The long, slender tusks of female elephants were considered the best for well-balanced balls. Until a suitable plastic substitute was invented, thousands of elephants died each year to supply the game rooms of Europe and America.

IVORY IN THE HIGHLANDS
Sometimes only a small part of a musical instrument was traditionally made with ivory, such as organ stops on church organs, ivory veneers on white piano keys, and the joints of this Highlander's bagpipes.

EXPENSIVE TOGGLES
Japanese *netsuke* are complete miniature sculptures. They were originally used as toggles on the end of purse strings, tied on to the belt of a kimono. Over the centuries, they became a collectible art form, and ivory was a popular material. This, and the even greater demand for ivory *hanko* (signature seals), made Japan the world's largest consumer of ivory before the trade was banned (p. 56).

This netsuke shows the old man who, according to Japanese legend, makes the cherry trees blossom

BANNED SOUVENIR TUSK
This tusk was bought as a souvenir and carefully carried home from an African holiday. Unfortunately for the tourist, who may not have known it was illegal, it was confiscated by customs officers. From its shape, we can deduce it came from a young bull elephant, probably in his teens, who was almost certainly killed by poachers. Only when tourists stop buying such souvenirs will poachers stop killing elephants to supply ivory for the tourist trade.

Sperm whale teeth are similar to elephant ivory when used for carving

Sperm whales are the biggest of the toothed whales

Sharp teeth, only in lower jaw, cut through squid

OFFSHORE SCRIMSHAW
During the long weeks at sea on 18th- and 19th-century whaling ships, some sailors passed the time by scratching pictures – usually of sailing ships and whales – onto the smoothed surface of sperm whale teeth, using a jack-knife or a sailmaker's needle.

BIG TEETH
Walrus, hippo, narwhal (a small whale), and various wild pigs all have teeth big enough to be of interest to ivory carvers, but strictly speaking only elephants produce true ivory. Nevertheless, when the ivory trade was banned, walrus poaching was reported to have increased in Alaska.

Walruses use their tusks for digging up shellfish from the seabed

Inuits (Eskimos) carved walrus tusks, which are enlarged canine teeth up to 3.3 ft (1 m) long

Trading elephant parts

M OST OF THE WORLD agreed to stop trading in ivory in 1989. This became law when the African elephant was listed, alongside the Asian species, on Appendix 1 of CITES, the Convention on International Trade in Endangered Species of Wild Fauna and Flora.

More than 115 countries have joined CITES, which limits or bans international trade in anything made from a species whose numbers are declining. The ivory ban was voted in because the estimated number of elephants in all Africa had fallen from 1.3 million in 1979 to 609,000 in 1989. At that rate, African elephants faced extinction within decades. But five southern African countries say they have so many elephants that they need to cull them (p. 61). They seek to sell ivory and elephant hides in a controlled trade which, they say, would help pay for conservation work. Most of the other 30 African countries with elephants object strongly, fearing a return of ivory poaching.

DO ELEPHANTS GRIEVE?
Between 70,000 and 100,000 elephants died every year during the 1980s to supply the world ivory trade. Up to 94 percent of those elephants were killed by poachers, the bodies left to rot and the calves left to die of starvation.

Ivory painted black for smuggling

SMUGGLERS' TRICKS
As long as there is some legal ivory on sale somewhere in the world, poached ivory will find a market. In 1991, a sharp-eyed Ugandan customs officer spotted a Korean businessman trying to smuggle ivory blocks, painted black to look like ebony, home to Korea, where selling ivory is still allowed.

Shoes made from elephant leather on sale in a Thai shop

ELEPHANT SHOES
Elephant leather also has a value, but in Africa poachers always take the tusks and leave the bulky hide to rot. In 1990, however, a trade in Asian elephant hides was exposed. They were smuggled out of Myanmar (Burma) into Thailand and sold as shoes and belts to tourists. Fortunately the exposé stopped most of the trade.

GET-RICH-QUICK GONE WRONG
Illegal ivory dealers tempt poverty-stricken African men with offers of a year's income for a few days' hunting. But in recent years, anti-poacher patrols have improved in many parts of Africa and poachers are more likely to end up behind bars. Unfortunately, the wealthy dealers who pay the poachers often escape the law. Since the ban, however, ivory prices have fallen and the trade is in decline.

ELEPHANT TABLETOP
The ban on ivory trading also prevents the sale of other elephant products outside the country of origin. In Zimbabwe or South Africa, a table topped by a layer of elephant skin such as this could be sold legally. But a tourist who bought one to take home to Europe or America would not be permitted to import it as long as elephants are on Appendix 1 of CITES.

Foot with a sturdy wood lining forms a hollow table leg for the tabletop (right)

ROUGH BANGLES
When ivory was fashionable, a large proportion of ivory products were made for women, either to wear as jewelry or to display in the home. Bangles were made from "bamboo ivory" – the hollow root of the tusk cut into slices.

Elephant hairs are still sold on traditional medicine stalls in some countries

WRONG-FOOTED
During the 19th century, big game hunters often returned from a safari with a set of tusks for the drawing room and an elephant's-foot umbrella stand or wastepaper bin. Because such products may still find a buyer, after a cull (p. 61) the elephant's feet are cut off and processed, adding to the value of the carcass.

THE FATE OF A CULLED ELEPHANT CARCASS
Nothing is wasted from a legally killed elephant in southern Africa: The meat is refrigerated or canned; the skin is made into leather for briefcases, cowboy boots, or tabletops; the tusks are carved into ornaments, and even the tail finds a market. Some tribes in Africa believe that a bracelet or ring made of elephant hair gives the owner something of the "force" of the elephant. Such bracelets became fashionable before public opinion turned against elephant products.

A day in the life

SMOOTH AS SILK
Skin care is important for elephants. A good scratch against a log, rock, or treetrunk will rub off the latest layer of dried mud as well as remove dead skin, ticks, and leeches.

ELEPHANTS APPEAR TO LEAD an enviable life, strolling along gently through an endless buffet restaurant, mingling with family and friends, courting, bringing up children, bathing, and taking a daily mudpack. Elephant life is certainly much more than one nonstop meal. At any time, feeding may be interrupted by socializing, travel, grooming, or resting. It is rare to come across elephants asleep, but they do sleep for a few hours in the early hours of the morning and again during the heat of the day, when they nap in the shade beneath any available tree. As a rule, only drought or human hunters are likely to shatter their easy existence.

EATING OUT
Studies of elephant activity-patterns in Uganda showed that there are three main feeding periods: in the morning, in the afternoon, and around midnight. Food items are selected largely by smell and touch, so feeding can easily continue into the night even if there is no moon.

CLAN GATHERING
Explorers' memoirs sometimes told of gatherings of thousands of elephants. Although such huge congregations are a thing of the past, neighboring herds of elephants do sometimes gather together for a few hours or a few days, only to split up and go their separate ways again afterward. No one knows why these gatherings take place.

THE YOUNG ONES
Young elephants who are getting all or a good portion of their food from mother's milk have time to spare. Instead of spending up to 80 percent of each day eating, they spend much of that time playing with their peers. Games can include chase-me, push-of-war, climb-up-the-playmate, or simply playing the fool.

DUST SHOWER
In the wild, self-dusting does not normally take much time out of each 24-hour cycle. In zoos, however, excessive dusting can become an abnormal behavior pattern, much as swaying from side to side and head bobbing often do. These are all signs of mental stress arising from boredom and an inadequate enclosure.

STILL IN TOUCH
People used to think that bull elephants spend a lot of their time alone. But the discovery that infrasonic elephant calls can travel over long distances suggests that even when out of sight of all other elephants, this bull will probably be part of a network of communicating elephants.

DAILY DRINKING SESSION
To a large extent, an elephant's life revolves around the water-holes in its home range. The distance to the nearest water-hole is always at the back of the matriarch's mind when she decides how far to forage for food.

CLOSE FAMILY TIES
Elephants make friends and reinforce family ties simply by spending time together, standing so close that they are often touching. Caressing with the trunk (and sniffing) is a part of it, as is a certain amount of gentle shoving. Sound is probably very important too: studies of the meaning of several infrasonic calls (p. 35) have revealed that certain calls have special meanings, some of which even seem to be directed toward a particular individual.

SUNDOWNERS
At the end of a long day of eating and socializing, what could be better than a long cool drink of water – particularly when home is the arid savanna of Etosha National Park, Namibia. Only the wetlands of the Etosha pan allow so many elephants and other large mammals to survive in this near-desert habitat.

Benevolent elephants

ELEPHANTS ARE DESCRIBED by ecologists as "keystone species." Ecology is the science concerned with ecosystems, the ways in which animals and plants interact with each other and with their environment. Elephants play such an important role in their ecosystem that, just as the removal of the central keystone in a stone arch causes it to collapse, so the loss of elephants from an area would cause the existing ecosystem to collapse. Many species of animals and plants, in both Africa and Asia, benefit from the presence of elephants. Some of these species could not survive without them. When conservationists try to protect elephants, their work has a wider aim as well – to save the whole ecosystem and preserve biodiversity (a wide range of species).

MOBILE WATCHTOWER
Cattle egrets often perch on elephants and dart between their legs, snapping up insects that fly up from under the feet of the walking elephants.

ELEPHANT WELL-DIGGERS
This young elephant is learning how to get a drink from a dried-up riverbed. With their tusks and trunk, elephants are well-equipped for digging. When rivers run dry during a drought, it is the elephants who dig down to find underground water sources. Once opened up by elephants, however, many other species will benefit from the newly exposed water hole.

FOREST MOTORWAYS
In areas of tangled forest or steep cliffs, traditional elephant pathways are the easiest way for most animals, including humans, to get around. Some pathways have been covered in tarmac to become roads for vehicles, though few drivers realize the debt they owe to past generations of elephants.

DUNG HARVEST
Rummaging around in a pile of elephant dung has its rewards for some animals, such as this baboon. Elephants have a rather inefficient digestive system, and some seeds that pass through undigested may be recycled as food for other animals.

Sometimes the weight of insects in elephant dung is more than the weight of the dung itself

SOWING FUTURE FORESTS
Many of the seeds that pass through an elephant undamaged will eventually germinate (grow). They have an ideal start in life, too, having been deposited in a neat package of elephant manure.

Acacia seed pods are a favorite food of many animals. Seeds do not germinate unless eaten by elephants or impalas. If eaten by baboons or vervet monkeys, the seeds are destroyed during digestion

Acacia seed pod

Acacia seed

Scarab beetles of the Heliocopris sp.

ELEPHANT DUNG PREFERRED
Elephants provide food for untold thousands of species of beetles, flies, worms, and other assorted dung-eating creatures. They, in turn, are food for a wide range of insect-eating animals. Most dung-eaters would probably be content with dung from any herbivore, but certain species of dung beetle are known to feed on and breed in elephant dung exclusively.

Most of these seeds and pods do not have an English name. Botanists give them Latin names. *Entada* sp. means a species in the genus *Entada*

Entada *sp.*

Mucuna *sp.*

Pentaclethra macrophylla

Dioclea *sp.*

Spondias *sp.*

Canavalia *sp.*

Arachis *sp.* (wild peanut)

Lecythidaceae sp.

Pods of *Bignoniaceae sp.*

This Congo pea pod is 33 in (83 cm) long

Acacia seed

Pods of Pentaclethra macrophylla *curl up as they dry*

SEEDS AND PODS

Little is known about the ecology of western African Congo-Guinean rainforests, but this collection of assorted seeds may contain species that are elephant-dependent. One study in the Tai Forest National Park in Ivory Coast, revealed that about one third of all the tree species whose seed dispersal mechanism was known, had their seeds spread by elephants. Some of those trees may have an economic value for timber, or for making traditional medicines. Therefore, saving the elephant is an important part of saving the rainforests.

In southern Africa, to prevent damage such as destruction of woodland, elephant numbers are controlled by culls, legally killing whole herds

TOO MANY ELEPHANTS?

Elephants often push trees down to feed on the upper branches. This is beneficial to smaller browsing animals that are otherwise unable to reach the top leaves. But if there are too many elephants crammed into a small park, the rate of tree destruction increases beyond the rate of new seedling growth. This converts woodland to grassland, which some people believe to be a bad thing.

SEED-STUDDED DUNG BALL

The flat-topped Acacia trees characteristic of East Africa have a problem. Weevils lay eggs in the seed pods, and the larvae destroy the seeds. But if an elephant (or an impala antelope) eats the pods, the weevil grub is digested and the seeds pass out in the animal's dung. Thus it is quite a common sight to see a crop of Acacia seedlings sprouting out of piles of decomposing elephant dung, sometimes miles away from the parent tree.

Saving the elephant

IF ELEPHANTS ARE TO SURVIVE, we must make sure that two things happen: First, enough elephant habitat must be left in a natural state. Elephants and people can share land, but the way we use that land must be compatible with elephant behavior and ecology. In savanna areas this could be mixed cattle and game ranching. In forests it could be selective logging (where only a few valuable trees are felled, leaving most of the forest intact). Secondly, the elephants must be protected. It is no use preserving their habitat if poachers are slaughtering the elephants. Since the 1989 ban on ivory (p. 56), poaching has declined, but talk of reopening the ivory trade in 1992 led to a resurgence in poaching. Everyone can help to stop this resurgence by refusing to buy ivory and protesting against its sale.

SAY IT WITH STICKERS
The campaign to ban the ivory trade won massive public support worldwide. In the United Kingdom alone, the conservation group Elefriends (p. 64) collected 1.5 million signatures. "Elefriendly zones," where ivory is not welcome, have been declared in many countries.

Drivers in natio... parks must he... the warning sig... elephants have... right of way!

ELEPHANT FUNERAL PYRE
On July 18, 1989, President Daniel T. arap Moi of Kenya put a torch to a bonfire of 12 tons of poached ivory. He joined Tanzania's call for an end to the ivory trade because Kenya had lost 85 percent of its elephants to poachers. Zambia, Dubai, Taiwan, and India have since followed Kenya's example, but hundreds of tons of ivory, mostly poached, remain in stockpiles around the world.

FRONT-LINE FORC...
Protecting wildlife is expensive... terms of money and lives. The bra... men of the anti-poaching patrols r... their lives daily in the war agai... poachers. Often they find themsel... in gun battles with poachers who... armed with automatic weapons l... over from civil wars or disband... armies. Refusing to buy ivory sav... human as well as elephant liv...

ELEPHANTS EARNING DOLLARS
Ecotourism (wildlife-watching holidays) can be a powerful force for conservation. However, it must be carefully controlled so that the tourists do not destroy the very species or habitat they wish to see. If a fair share of the profits from tourism is directed into the local community, then the community will also value its wildlife and not turn to poaching for money.

Scientists keep track of the elephants' movements by fitting radio collars onto them

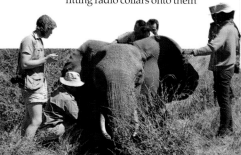

RADIO ELEPHANT
Many national parks were designated by a line drawn on a map, setting off an area of little use to people. But problems ensue if park borders cut across animal migration routes. By fitting radio collars onto elephants, scientists can find out where they roam and then change park boundaries or make "corridors" from one park to another.

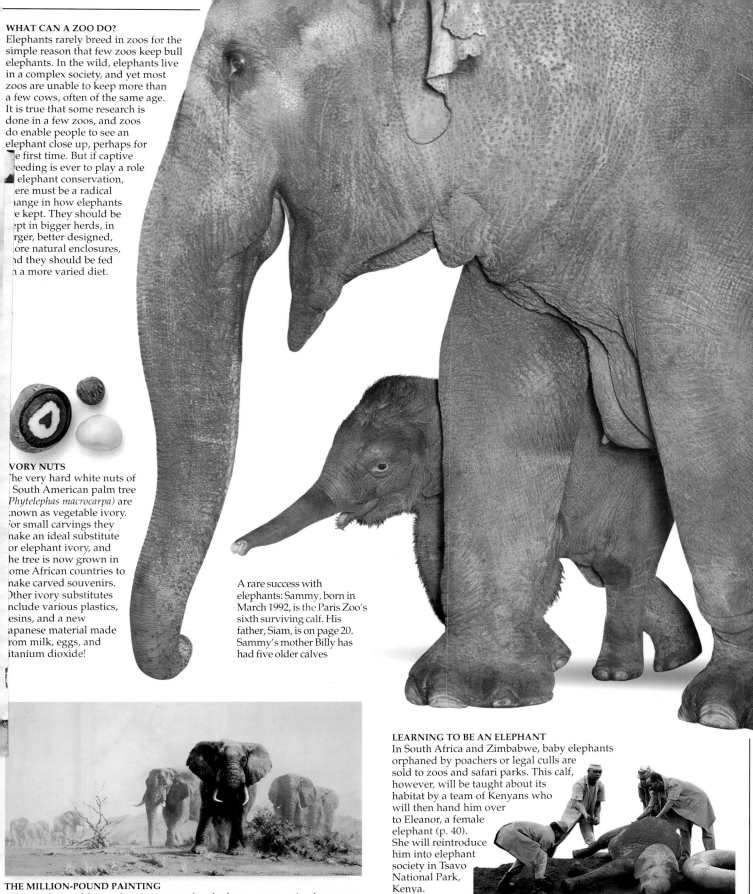

WHAT CAN A ZOO DO?

Elephants rarely breed in zoos for the simple reason that few zoos keep bull elephants. In the wild, elephants live in a complex society, and yet most zoos are unable to keep more than a few cows, often of the same age. It is true that some research is done in a few zoos, and zoos do enable people to see an elephant close up, perhaps for the first time. But if captive breeding is ever to play a role in elephant conservation, there must be a radical change in how elephants are kept. They should be kept in bigger herds, in larger, better designed, more natural enclosures, and they should be fed on a more varied diet.

IVORY NUTS

The very hard white nuts of a South American palm tree (*Phytelephas macrocarpa*) are known as vegetable ivory. For small carvings they make an ideal substitute for elephant ivory, and the tree is now grown in some African countries to make carved souvenirs. Other ivory substitutes include various plastics, resins, and a new Japanese material made from milk, eggs, and titanium dioxide!

A rare success with elephants: Sammy, born in March 1992, is the Paris Zoo's sixth surviving calf. His father, Siam, is on page 20. Sammy's mother Billy has had five older calves

THE MILLION-POUND PAINTING

All over the world, people raise money for elephant conservation by means of sponsored walks, swims, recitals, and many other activities. Perhaps the most ambitious is British wildlife artist David Shepherd (p. 64). Through sales of prints of his painting "The Ivory is Theirs," he was two thirds of the way toward his target of two million dollars by mid-1992.

LEARNING TO BE AN ELEPHANT

In South Africa and Zimbabwe, baby elephants orphaned by poachers or legal culls are sold to zoos and safari parks. This calf, however, will be taught about its habitat by a team of Kenyans who will then hand him over to Eleanor, a female elephant (p. 40). She will reintroduce him into elephant society in Tsavo National Park, Kenya.

Index

Acknowledgments

Dorling Kindersley would like to thank:
The elephant keepers at Howlett's
and Port Lympne Wildlife Parks, and
at Whipsnade Wild Animal Park; Parc
Zoologique de Paris; Jane Pickering at the
Oxford University Museum; Dr Palmer
and Dr. R. M. Owens of the National
Museum of Wales; Elephant Interest
Group, and Jeheskel Shoshani for
checking text (pp. 8–9, 10–11, 14–15)
and for trunk references (p. 19);
Ashley Leiman; Dr Evison of the
Bodleian Library;
Editorial assistance: Helena Spiteri.
Design assistance: Manisha Patel,
Sharon Spencer.
Research assistance: Céline Carez.
Photographic assistance: Jonathan
Buckley. Illustrations: Joanna Cameron.
Index: Jane Parker. Additional
photography: Geoff Brightling (p. 61)

Elefriends, 162 Boundaries Road, London
SW12 8HG;
David Shepherd Conservation
Foundation, PO BOX 123, Godalming,
Surrey GU8 4JS

Picture credits
t=top, b=bottom, c=center, l=left, r=right

Cover: Bodleian Library; Bruce Coleman
Ltd./M. Freeman; MEPL; OSF/M. Colbeck

Amnistie Pour Les Eléphants/The East
African Wildlife Society, Japan/Elefriends/
Humane Society of USA: 62tl;
Bridgeman Art Library/Albertina Graphic
Collection, Vienna: 53tl/Bibliothèque
Nationale, Paris: 52tr/Anthony Crane
Collection: 50cl/National Library of
Scotland: 47cla/Private Collection: 27clb/
Victoria & Albert Museum: 21cl, 47bc;
Bodleian Library, Oxford: 46br, 48cra;
Camera Press: 47bl/M. Amin: 56bl/
D. Anthony: 17bl/H. Miller: 41cl/
B.G. Silberstein: 45tl/Chester Zoo: 39b, 51br;
Bruce Coleman Ltd: 26b/J. & D. Bartlett:
59tl, 59br/J. Burton: 18tr/A. Compost: 24tr,
25cla, 28cla/G. Cubitt: 25cra, 27b, 62tr/P.
Davey: 28bl, 32c/A.J. Deane: 56clb/J. Foott:
33tl/M. Freeman: 28tl, 58bl/G. Hessler: 13tl/
Dr. M.P. Kahl: 17cla/F. Lanting: 13bl/L. Lee
Rue: 31 cra/Dr. N. Myers: 39 cla/D. & M.
Plage 28cr, 31 bl, 36bl, 45 crb/Dr. E. Pott:
52tl/P. Price: 13cr/S. Trevor: 7tl/G. Ziesler:
37bl/C. Zuber: 37br/38 cra;
Environmental Picture Library/
R. Hadley: 62bl;
FLPA/F. Hartmann: 29bl, 60tl, 60cla, 60cb,
62c/F.W. Lane: 13br/L. Lee Rue: 27tl/P.
Perry: 17bc, 27cr/R. Prickett: 42cr/M.B.
Withers: 21ca;
Robert Harding : 7b, 33b, 51cra;
Michael Holford: 49bl/British Museum: 54tl,
54bl/Victoria & Albert Museum: 33tr, 54br,
55cl;
Hutchison Library: 48br/John Hatt: 6tr;
Images Colour Library: 49cl;
Images of Africa/David Keith Jones: 40bl,
40br/Carla Signorini Jones: 39cr;
Imperial War Museum, London: 47cra;
Jacana: 7tr;
Kobal Collection/MGM: 51tl;
Roger Lee: 55tl;
Mary Evans: 7cr, 26tl, 32tl, 47br, 48tl, 50tr,
54c/Mansell Collection: 55tr;
Musée Nationale d'Histoire Naturelle,
Paris: 10cla;
Nature Photographers/H. Van Lawick: 35bl;
N.H.M, London: 9c, 9cr, 10bc;
NHPA/A. Bannister: 32bl, 58c, 61br/M.
Danegger: 22tl/K. Ghani: 45br/P. Johnson:
31br/J. Shaw: 13tr, 32br/K. Switak: 60bl;
Robert Opie Collection: 40tl;
OSF/43tl/R. Ben Shahar: 45cra, 56tl/
M.J. Coe: 62br/M. Colbeck: 30ca, 30cbr, 33c,
40c, 58bl, 59tr/J. Foott: 12bl/
G. Thompson: 25tl/E. Sadd 42cl;
Planet Earth Pictures/S.T. Avery: 42bl/I.
Douglas-Hamilton: 41bl/J. Downer: 21tr/
J. Scott: 41br;
Ian Redmond:18br, 18bc, 18cr, 19tcl, 21cla,
23br, 25br, 27tr, 29tr, 30bl, 35cl, 39cl, 41cra,
43cra, 43clb, 56cla, 58cla, 59crb, 60cra, 60clb,
62cra, 63br;
Rhodes House Library, Oxford: 21tl;
The Royal Armouries, London 46bl;
A. Sutcliffe: 43tr;
David Shepherd Conservation Foundation/
WWF UK: 63bl;
Survival Anglia/B. Davidson: 31tl;
Victoria & Albert Museum: 45 tr;
Illustration from WINNIE-THE-POOH
copyright E.H. Shepard under the Berne
Convention, in the USA copyright 1926 by
E.P. Dutton & Co Inc, renewal 1954 by
A.A. Milne. Colouring in copyright © 1973
by E.H. Shepard and Methuen Children's
Books Ltd: 51 tr;
Zoo Atlanta: 41tl

Every effort has been made to trace the
copyright-holders. Dorling Kindersley
apologises for any unintentional omissions
and would be pleased, in such cases, to add
an acknowledgement in future editions.